Finding Home

EMBRACING GOD'S PROMISES AND REBUILDING YOUR LIFE

SYBIL KOLBERT

Contents

Introduction   ix

1. Before The Words   1

   Empty   5
2. Rebuilding Begins With A Burden   7

   Overwhelmed   23
3. Opportunity For Change   25

   Breathe   41
4. Evaluate The Rubble   43

   Deep   55
5. Rebuilding In Community   57

   Remember   77
6. Work + Fight Go Together   79

   Believe   91
7. Rebuilding Reveals Vulnerability + Hope   93

   Boundary   105
8. Embrace Limits + Celebrate   107

   Freedom   123
9. Remembering Leads To Surrender   125

   Stand   135
10. New Beginnings + Commitments   137

   Behold   149
11. Rebuilding Is Ongoing + We Are Being Built   151

12. Final Words + Words Yet To Come   165

   Reflection + Study Guide Questions   171
   Notes   177
   Additional Resources   181

For my parents, grandparents, and the others who have come before me:
You have helped shape my faith.

For my husband and children:
Your unconditional love, patience, and support are the reason this book exists.

Introduction

They say, "Home is where the heart is."

I disagree.

What if it's more than that? What if home is the place where your heart *and* soul reside? The place where your deepest desires, burdens, and commitments meet the most fundamental part of who you are. The most distinct, authentic part of you— e.g., your love of learning, deep belly laugh, empathetic nature, slow pace, etc. Together, the heart and soul form the part of you that belongs simply because it is who God created you to be.

Home is where I've always longed to be. I'm what some may call a "homebody." As a kid, I said "no" to many sleepovers and slumber parties. I preferred staying home where I felt safe and comfortable even though the world was still scary. It was where I felt seen as my true self, where the most fundamental things about me remained true, and where I knew I belonged.

The more I've thought about home, the more I've realized that although it can be about safety and comfort, it's more about being secure in our identity and belonging. It's about who we are and our ability to act authentically. I'm most at home when

I'm living out of the core part of who I am, the deepest, most authentic part.

Finding home has been a journey for me. I wonder if it has been for you as well.

How do we find home?

By reaching in and finding our souls.

Unfortunately, finding home often involves losing it first or never having experienced it in the first place. Our need for home doesn't show up on a lit-up path like the lights of an airport runway or through experiences decorated with rainbows and sunshine. It's often through loss and burden, suffering and despair. Through falling down and getting up again. Over and over. The breaking apart and the putting back together. Sometimes we find home. And other times, we rebuild it.

We know home as a place, space, or group of people who allow you to be yourself and who allow you to showcase your God-given skills, strengths, gifts, and character. Not to earn praise, accolades, or validation but to feel alive and settled. It's where you and I can know and live that which is fundamentally and ontologically true about ourselves as we bring glory to God and promote the good of those around us. To find this home, though, we must first discover a different one, one that we can only begin to experience in this life but will extend into eternity. This home is one only God can provide with His presence and our commitment to dwelling in the abode that He had designed for us.

This book is about rebuilding. It contains my stories and the story of God's people rebuilding as they make their way home again. As you read, you may discover that the format differs from what you expect of books like this.

It was important to me to share my story alongside and blended together with the story of scripture, primarily found in the book of Nehemiah. However, we will explore other scripture as well. Our stories partner with God's story. Finding and rebuilding our home finds its foundation in whom God has created us to be, His Word, and His pattern of taking His people through rebuilding as essential to our process. Take advantage of the reflection questions in the back of the book and share your journey with someone you can trust.

Through my own story and the narrative of scripture, I have discovered that home is where our stories matter but don't define us. Why? Because God defines us and created us for a purpose. It's God who promised the opportunity for rebuilding. It's not until we find our home in His presence that we can really find our home. I pray this book will challenge you to step outside your ideas of *home* and into how God defines *home* for you.

Friend, who is it that God has created you to be? Where or with whom do you feel the most at home?

If you are struggling to answer these questions, don't panic. I've decided to go first, to be vulnerable with the ways God has spoken into my story of rebuilding so that you can find *your* home as you read. I share my own journey of finding home, not just once, but multiple times. After a struggle with postpartum depression and a crisis of faith, I had to find my way back to myself. After leaving a career I'd spent much of my life working toward, I was forced to rediscover my identity. Then, in the midst of a health crisis, I was given a chance to rebuild my life into something new, coming closer to myself than I'd ever been —again. Finding and rebuilding are life themes of mine, but also of God's people... including you.

If you feel like you've yet to find home, this book is for you. If you feel like you've lost the only home you've ever known, this book is for you. If home feels messy and confusing and you'd rather run from it than find it, this book is for you. Wherever you find yourself, you have my permission to begin a new journey of searching and rebuilding. My prayer is that you will ultimately find your home in God.

ONE

Before The Words

HAVE you ever felt like God is writing more than one story for your life? One with pain, suffering, and wilderness experiences and one full of redemption, joy, and an overwhelming sense of His presence?

This is exactly how I've felt as I've wrestled with feelings of depression and heaviness that seemed too great to bear—and also experienced abundant joy and provision.

The first story I wanted to put down on these pages was the easier one—the one that was full of God's kindness and generous provision. It was a beautiful story of how God lifted me from despair and striving and called me back to Himself with His still, small voice. I like this story.

But God also asked me to write down the other story. It wasn't a story I wanted to look at, let alone write down—the physical pain, the weight fluctuation, and the feelings of utter hopelessness I've cycled through over the past ten years. Out of reluctant obedience, I re-read my journals and sat once again in the experiences I would've rather forgotten—so that I could write them down, for you and me.

The journey that God has had me on over the past ten years

is sometimes inexplicable. I have experienced restlessness and certainty, bold faith and doubt, despair, and hope. Yet, God was the constant amid these ever-changing emotions and unexpected and uncertain circumstances. He was the variable that never changed.

Both narratives, side-by-side, tell the story of how God moved. How He prepared, sustained, and propelled me forward. How He speaks, comforts, and inspires. How He gives and takes away, loving me through it all. Helping me to be braver than I ever thought I could be, even through experiencing the loss of normalcy and control.

This is the story of rebuilding. Of finding home. From captivity to freedom. From burden to celebration.

The wall of my closet holds my whole story—at least the story up to this point. It's not necessarily the story I would have chosen. It's God's story in me.

I enter my closet and look to the right. Above a shelf with numerous sweatshirts is the wall with words, photos, quotes, and verses. Each is a marker representing a point in time over the past ten years—my years of rebuilding.

The words form an arc and are held together by a single thread. They are the words God has used to guide and grow me along this decade's journey toward a greater understanding of myself through a bigger vision of Him.

Although each of these words holds a separate meaning, looking back, I can see their connection—how God has woven them together and created a path that has led me home.

These words and phrases have confused and inspired me. They have been some of the easiest and hardest things to hear.

You may wonder how God gave me these words or what it's like to *hear* Him. For me, it's like an urgent feeling or sense that I get. It usually begins with a word or thought in my mind. Then, as I read, study the Bible, have conversations, etc., the concept continues to show up. So much so that I know it has to be from God. I have learned that this is His way of speaking to me.

If you haven't heard from God, don't worry, I haven't always heard Him either. Or at least, I didn't believe I did. However, what is more likely is that He was speaking, but I didn't recognize His voice among the cacophony of other voices that bombarded me daily. Even today, when I struggle to hear God, it's because I am too busy or preoccupied. And, if I am completely honest, I have often thought that it was weird or fanatical to say that God had spoken to me. That is, until the spring of 2012.

After that? Well, that is a whole different story.

Empty

DEFINITION

Containing nothing; not occupied or inhabited. Lacking reality, substance, meaning, or value: hollow.

A DEEPER LOOK

To be filled, we must first be empty, having withheld nothing. Release yourself so that you can be filled with more of God. To know more of Him. To be more like Him. Come to God with open hands—empty to be filled.

VERSE

"Unless the Lord builds the house, the builders labor in vain. Unless the Lord watches over the city, the guards stand watch in vain" (Psalm 127:1).

TWO

Rebuilding Begins With A Burden

I REMEMBER JANUARY 11, 2014, very clearly.

Sitting in a parked car in a church parking lot, my insides shook, and my mouth was dry. Only 30 minutes remained before I was due to go on stage, but I couldn't move. I refused to open the door. What had I been thinking?

My husband, Matt, who had driven me to the church, gently reminded me that I couldn't stay in the car and be on stage simultaneously. I had committed and had to follow through. To do that, my presence was required... in the church sanctuary.

Finally, out of the car and into the church, I took my assigned seat in the front row with several others who had been given the same task—to read letters we'd written to various categories of women, particularly wives. The keynote speaker was Jennifer Smith. She was the one who'd invited me here and provided this opportunity to share my thoughts and encouragement with the weary wife.

As was typical when I was in church, my notebook lay open on my lap. I listened and took notes as Jennifer spoke about light and longing. *What is it I am longing for?* I sang along as the worship team led us in song and listened as a few other letter-writing women were introduced and read their letters to the crowd of more than 500.

I was sure someone had turned up the heat in the church. My body felt hot, and my face felt like the same shade of red as my shirt. I couldn't imagine getting up on that stage and speaking without throwing up. My turn was coming quickly. I said a silent prayer and knew Matt was in the back of the church doing the same.

My legs trembled as I walked toward the front of the sanctuary and onto the stage. Once I stood behind the podium, the strangest thing happened. Even though I was still shaking inside, my voice came out clear and calm over the microphone. I read my letter with poise and passion. And when I stepped off the stage, I was energized, feeling more alive than I'd felt in a long time. *When do I get to do that again?* I wondered.

Months before I set foot on that stage, I had begun to feel unresolved, restless, and like I was meant for something new, something more. I felt as if God had been giving me new passions and gifts while the passions from the years before, the areas I thought I'd been called to, gradually faded. So much so that they had become draining rather than energizing. It was hard to imagine that the people, places, and things I had devoted my adult life to could feel lifeless and uninspiring.

It was Matthew 5:6, the verse that Jennifer shared that morning, the lyrics from *Oceans* by Hillsong, one of the songs the worship team led, and the feelings of restlessness that were unfamiliar and impossible to ignore that taught me to pray new prayers for 2014 and beyond.

Father, I want to be known as a woman who hungers and thirsts after You, Your righteousness. Jesus, call me into the deep, to the unknown. Spirit, lead me where my trust is without borders.

What I noticed most about myself then was that as I opened

myself up to more of what God wanted for my life, as I held space empty of expectations and assumptions, I could carry Him with me. As I approached God with open-handed surrender, He began to fill me with more than I could've ever imagined.

The more I searched for Him, the more I found of Him. The more I stewarded the gifts He had given me, the more generous He was. It was amazing and awe-inspiring, and I wanted more of it!

If you had known me before 2012, you wouldn't have truly known me. And I would've liked it that way.

For many years I said *no*. No to freedom. No to passion. No to abundance. Looking back, I wasn't even aware I was doing it. I didn't know any better. I wasn't ready. Because who would knowingly refuse any of these things?

I did. In doing so, I was also saying *no* to knowing God and allowing Him to work in and through me.

Why? Because most of the time, saying *yes* didn't make sense. I'm the kind of person that likes things to make sense.

I'm not saying that I didn't pray or attempt to discover God's path for my life. I did. I had a life that pleased me and was safe and comfortable. I did good things. I was a good person. But I wasn't living a life of complete surrender. My joy was not complicated or courageous.

It wasn't until the spring of 2012, when I was heavily burdened, desperate for answers, and weary from all I had tried that hadn't worked, that I started to make room to hear from God. I began to listen for His still, small voice. Before 2012, the competing voices of fear, doubt, pride, and perfectionism had been too strong. They interfered with my ability to hear Him, receive, and take action.

It wasn't until I began my journey of rebuilding, with small steps of courage and faith, that I began to see how captive I had been to the noise produced by those other voices.

I have often wondered what words I missed before April

2012. Had He been speaking to me all along, and I just hadn't been listening? I was sad for all of Him I had missed but excited to realize that I could listen more intently now and start fresh. He wouldn't be disappointed in me because He loved me today, just as He had from day one.

From 2012 until now, God has been with me in the lowest valleys, pushing me to new heights. He has given wings to my words, or rather, to *His* words.

FINDING HOME IN JERUSALEM

Much like my story—and I'm guessing yours, too—the story of the people of Israel includes struggle, hardship, loss, and brokenness. They were driven from their cities by their enemies and forced to live among their enemy nations for nearly seven decades.

What is also a part of their story is a God who, not long into their exile, promised them rebuilding, only to make way for it 70 years later. Beyond their seasons of struggle and brokenness, God made way for rebuilding.

When the time came for rebuilding, two groups of exiles returned to Jerusalem and, after more than fifty years, had rebuilt the temple—the place they believed God resided. Zerubbabel led the first group of rebuilders, and Ezra, a priest and scribe, led the second. Together, these two groups had rebuilt the temple but left Jerusalem's city walls untouched and the city itself largely uninhabited.

There are many possible reasons why these two groups decided not to continue rebuilding. If we assume chapter four of Ezra is out of chronological order, the people of Israel likely stopped rebuilding due to a decree issued by the King of Persia, one of the nearby nations.

Let's use our biblical imagination and consider a few other scenarios that could also be true:

1. The people got busy with their own lives, families, and responsibilities;
2. They became discontent, frustrated by all of the resistance and attacks from the other nations, and began doubting the goodness of God and His ability to provide;
3. They were distracted by the prettier and well-built cities and nations surrounding them and began to desire what they saw.

No matter the reason, some of the brokenness remained. God's promise spoken through the prophet Jeremiah that the city's wall would be rebuilt had not yet been fulfilled. The burden of the broken wall remained.

FINDING HOME THROUGH BURDEN

Similar to the Israelites, I experienced the burden of brokenness and partially built pieces of life, too. My earliest burdens weren't the result of crisis or sin but self-doubt and a fractured identity.

When I was a young girl, I had one prayer that I still remember with clarity. Each night before I went to sleep, I prayed that I would have long, straight hair instead of my short, curly hair. Yet, despite how earnest I had been in my prayers the night before, I still looked the same every morning. I can't remember how many nights I prayed this prayer, but eventually, I stopped.

My hair is red and curly. It always has been. Think little orphan Annie. You know, "The sun will come out tomorrow..."? My hair is the one physical trait that made me stand out. As a child, I got comments—sometimes unkind—from everyone. Until early adulthood, I hated it!

Didn't God see that I didn't look like the other girls I knew? Didn't He see how much I hated being different?

I had big faith as a child to believe that this change could happen overnight or that it was even possible at all. If anyone could change the length and texture of my hair in just one night, it was God, right? I was desperate and dissatisfied. And I was only eight years old.

Although noteworthy in my childhood memory, this unanswered prayer was insignificant compared to what I believe was my most significant crisis of faith.

I made my first commitment to Jesus in the open areas of a local park, surrounded by dozens of other kids. I was seven.

Between that day and what came almost thirty years later were years of circumstances, relationships, and spiritual disciplines—the building blocks of my faith. Yet, when the devastating blow of what I now believe was postpartum depression consumed me, my faith wasn't ready—it shattered, sending pieces of what I thought I believed in a million different directions. My faith was bent, bruised, and broken. Fortunately, it had not been destroyed. A remnant remained.

Our circumstances often bring to light what we already think about God. We may say we trust, but without the opportunity to show our trust, a life of faith can become compulsory and rote. We only see our faith's true strength—or lack—when the circumstances demand it.

During my faith crisis, the postpartum depression had spilled over into a messy and disordered life. I had three children under six, and my youngest had needs I couldn't keep up with. I was exhausted and, again, began to believe that God didn't see me. *Surely, if He could see the struggle, He would do something to fix it. Right?*

I was burdened for myself and my son. There was something different about him. It was more than the sleepless nights and the challenges of being the parent of a newborn, a toddler, and a soon-to-be kindergartener. Depression crept in and wasn't leaving. Doubt about my skills as a mother was at an all-time high.

Doubt about whom God was bubbled beneath the surface. I didn't believe that my prayers mattered, that they would change anything. Therefore, I couldn't pray. Emptiness engulfed me. The heaviness of the burden was there, but my desire and ability to pray had disappeared.

When I think about it now, I wonder if it wasn't my confidence in prayer that had waned but my trust in the God who had provided prayer as a way of calling out and listening to Him. I didn't believe God was listening all the nights I cried myself to sleep. I wasn't eager to hear what He had to say about me, my son, or my circumstances. And I certainly wasn't experiencing His presence.

When I finally got the courage to talk to Matt about my doubts, lack of confidence, reluctance, and inability to pray, he was concerned. And, rightly so. As was true to his brand, he desired to fix it. But I didn't know how it could be fixed, nor did he. Soon after our conversation, he went to our pastor and long-time friend, looking for solutions. There were none, at least nothing specific, besides continuing to pray *for* me and for *me*.

Unbeknownst to me, I had others praying for me during that time too. Friends from church, family, etc. They didn't know the extent or details of my struggle. But they knew enough. The prayers of others truly got me through that long season.

When I didn't know how to have faith, they did. When I didn't believe that God could see me, they believed *for* me.

FINDING HOME IN JERUSALEM

In 538 B.C., when the Persian government overthrew the Babylonians, the Persian king issued a decree which allowed all Jews to return from exile.[1] However, some Jewish people decided to remain in the lands of their exile. One of those people was Nehemiah. He remained in Susa in the palace of the Persian

King Artaxerxes, living a life of prestige and influence as a member of the king's court.

The book of Nehemiah begins with Nehemiah's first-person account of his inquiry about the current conditions of Jerusalem —his city and its people. Even though he lived and worked in Susa, Nehemiah's ancestors were from Jerusalem; Nehemiah was an Israelite.

The Israelites were God's chosen people. Their nation began with one man God had called out of his homeland and into a life of faith. This man would become the father of a nation extending through generations. God chose His people not based on their merit or character but on His own. Despite their many flaws, God called them to live in His presence and be blameless (Genesis 17:1). He set them apart as a great nation and secured them an inheritance. He would be their God, and they would be His people.

As the nation of Israel increased and multiplied in number, they became a threat to the authorities in Egypt and were enslaved there.

After 400 years of brutal treatment and oppressive working conditions, God brought them out of slavery. He took the Hebrew people into the wilderness, where they spent 40 years, with the Lord's provision sustaining them day by day.

At the appointed time, God brought His people into a place of abundance and gave them an inheritance of land eternal and spoke this over them:

> I will dwell among the Israelites and be their God. And
> they will know that I am the Lord their God, who
> brought them out of the land of Egypt so that I might
> dwell among them. I am the Lord their God (Exodus
> 29:45-46, CSB).

In their new home, God drew their boundary lines, both

literally and metaphorically, giving each group or tribe a location to dwell and rules. At first glance, these rules and boundaries appeared to be about limits but were actually about love
and order and justice. These guidelines provided the people
with instructions on how to love God as Lord and King, to love
each other, and to preserve the dignity of the poor and
oppressed.

God walked alongside His people, even as they did what was
evil in His sight. He raised judges as deliverers and, after many
more years, acquiesced to the people's requests for a king.

The Israelites claimed to love God yet wanted to be like the
other nations. Their identity was special and distinct, but they
resisted living in it for generations because it was different. The
people built themselves and their nation upon the wrong things.
Their loyalty should have been to the God who had brought
them out of slavery, yet they betrayed Him by looking to the
other nations and their gods for satisfaction.

After many years of disloyalty to God, brokenness, and struggle, the people of Israel were completely overtaken by their
enemies. They were relocated, sent away from their homes, and
forced to live in unfamiliar lands for many generations.

While living in these unfamiliar places, some people were
reeducated, given new ways to live and new customs and rules
to follow; they began to blend in with the people around them.
Others held onto their identity as God's chosen despite living
and working for the good of the towns to which they were
exiled.

Just as with their slavery, oppression, and years of wandering, God had promised His people a way forward; their time to
return home would come. He would preserve a remnant, and
they would have a chance to rebuild.

Nehemiah's story began long before his inquiry into the
state of Jerusalem and its people. Despite being a member of the
Persian king's court, Nehemiah's identity remained distinct and

was secured in his relationship with his God; he was a Hebrew and cared about his people and their future.

Nehemiah became burdened when he heard of the ruin still present in the land and with the people. His natural response to his own pain and the suffering of his people was to pray. Nehemiah mourned, prayed, and fasted for four months before deciding to ask his boss, the king, for a leave of absence as the cupbearer.

Nehemiah was sad and afraid, yet he moved forward with well-placed confidence; his trust lay in God from the very beginning.

FINDING HOME THROUGH BURDEN

I walked out into my backyard one spring afternoon just after a rainstorm. The branches of all of our Japanese maple trees were drooping. Even the strongest and heaviest branches appeared pushed toward the ground under the weight of the water. Drips of moisture fell to the ground, like tears into a puddle. They were not broken, just weighed down.

The burden and intensity of the rain had been too much for the branches to carry. They desperately needed the water, especially after many years of drought in California. The water would produce good in them—bringing nutrients to the soil, strengthening their roots, and producing fruit for their branches. But on the cool spring afternoon, the water was too heavy. It seemed like too much.

The beauty of it struck me—the pushing and weeping that would lead to flourishing. With the right conditions and proper care, this Japanese maple would be at home again in our yard. The branches would recover their buoyancy; the tree would thrive again.

Rebuilding begins with a burden. Something has changed, gone wrong, or been lost.

Although the beginning of my story with God involved me taking my burden to Him, when my seasons of pain and suffering became too great, I often chose a different path—one of withdrawal, doubt, and disconnection.

In contrast, Nehemiah's burden led him straight to God. He was compelled by compassion to be part of the solution and knew that he needed God to do it. Nehemiah's response is evidence of his confidence in God and commitment to endure in His plan.

Nehemiah emptied himself of his own agenda, making space for God to move and do what only He could do in his life and in the heart of the king.

LOOKING BACK, I can see that God had a pattern of revealing words to me. He would begin speaking to me in various ways in the fall of one year and continue until I was certain it was His word and His vision, not mine. The second time it happened was in the fall of 2014. I was attending a women's retreat at Hume Lake Christian Camps.

Between the years of fighting with depression that turned into a crisis of faith and leaving my job in education was a new request from God—to be a conduit of connection between the women in my sphere of influence and to connect them with Him.

It had been years since a group of women from our church had attended the women's retreat at Hume Lake. A small group returned in 2013—an even bigger group in the fall of 2014.

As the leader and organizer of the group, I was tasked with confirming registrations and organizing carpools. In addition to taking care of the logistics, I felt inspired to prepare a letter and gift for all the women in my group. Each one received a journal, pen, and a note of encouragement I had prayed over. On the front cover of their journals was a sticker that had been custom-made. It said, "Make today's story a great one." I was intrigued by my own story then and believed every person's story was significant. I wanted the women to believe that their stories mattered too.

In my letter, I asked the women to consider their part in God's story and to surrender their story to God, its author, making space for Him to move. Imagine my surprise when on the first night of camp, the speaker spoke a challenge from the stage; she asked us to view God as the writer, director, and producer of a grand story. To recognize that He is the central main character. And to ask, "What is my part in God's story?"

I was speechless, but my mind was racing. My mouth hung open. My body paralyzed with wonder. *How could this have happened?* God had given me this message months before. He guided me toward it, shaped it, and used me to bring it to the women of my group.

God provided me with a gift that night. The burden God had given me for women who feel disconnected, weary, or anxious, was not only because it was where I had been but because it was where I still was. I needed His encouragement. God saw the need, and He came through.

I felt important. Not because I possessed some special knowledge or connection with God. I felt important *to* God, like I belonged to Him. In His kindness, He had let me know—in no small way—that He knew me, saw me, and loved me. I felt a bit like Job toward the end of his conversation with God about hardship and blessing:

> I admit I once lived by rumors of you; now I have it all
> firsthand—from my own eyes and ears! (Job 42:5,
> MSG).

I sat in the chapel, surrounded by hundreds of women, yet

felt like He was speaking directly to me. I was overwhelmed by the truth of God's sovereignty. I was undone by His loving kindness toward me. He had chosen me to lead these women to Him, speak into their lives, and give evidence that He is alive and active. To make Him known as the Author and Perfecter of our faith, of the story He was writing in their lives.

I knew I wanted more of whatever *this* was. My desire was to be overwhelmed by Him. There it was, my word for 2015: *Overwhelmed*.

There are many things in life that burden or overwhelm us. Many of them are external, meaning they come from outside of us. Things like conflict in relationships or challenges with physicians and insurance companies, workplace or home stressors, etc. Some internal states or emotions can overwhelm. Shame is one of them.

Shame appears early in the Bible, within the narrative of Genesis 3. Sin is introduced to the reader in that chapter through Adam and Eve's disobedience. After they sinned, Adam and Eve felt guilt and shame; in response, they covered themselves with leaves and hid from God in the garden. When God came to find them, He freed them from their shame and released their guilt with a sacrifice. He also devised a rescue and restoration plan for the future—for us. That plan was Jesus.

Those who were a part of Jesus' earthly family are listed in Matthew 1:1-16. As we read through that list, included are a few names we may not expect. Among the men listed, there are also five women: two widows (one mistreated and the other an immigrant), a prostitute, a victim of sexual assault, and an unwed teenager who became pregnant.

All of these women's stories were impacted by sin. Each held the shame of their stories and of being seen as unworthy and vulnerable. Yet, they were chosen by God to be a part of His plan to send Jesus into the world. The same world that hated them would also hate Him.

In John 15:1, Jesus said, "I am the true vine..." This was significant to His original audience because they knew that the vine metaphor was often used to describe Israel as the vine of the past, the vine that had been loved and cared for by God only to yield bad fruit (Isaiah 5:1-5, CSB). Jesus calling Himself the true vine removed the banner of failure from Israel; it removed their guilt and shame.

Shame takes sin—either our own or that which has been done to us—and puts it at the center of who we are. But from the beginning to the end, God has made a way for His people to know that it is not sin or shame that defines them. It is God who defines us. We are not living to *achieve* an identity. We are living to match an identity we've already been given.

Even though your shame may tempt you to hide from God, He will come near to you. God does not want you to withdraw or hide from the sin in your life because of shame. He is not mad at you or disappointed in you. In fact, it is in the presence of sin where God's love and grace are the most needed and abundant!

Finding home after seasons of struggle and despair is not just about rebuilding our lives but also our home in God.

If we allow God to provide us with our vision for rebuilding and partner with Him in the process, He will give us the ability to change our perspectives, increase our faith, and find our hope once again. In the post-New Testament era, this is possible because of Jesus. Because He has made room for us. In Jesus, we live and move and have our being (Acts 17:28).

Although Nehemiah didn't know Jesus, He *did* know God as the holy, sovereign, loving, and faithful Lord of Heaven and Earth. He believed in the God who had promised to take His people home, proclaimed the message "change is possible," and was present through it all.

See, we count as blessed those who have endured. You have

heard of Job's endurance and have seen the outcome
that the Lord brought about—the Lord is compas-
sionate and merciful (James 5:11, CSB).

This was the God who lifted Nehemiah's burden—the same One who has lifted mine and can lift yours.

Overwhelmed

DEFINITION

Upset or overthrow; to cover over completely. To overpower in thought or feeling.

A DEEPER LOOK

To be overwhelmed by God's presence. To experience more of His kindness and favor. To notice too much of God, seeing Him everywhere and in everything. To be weighed down by the miraculous work of the Holy Spirit and undone by God's love, grace, goodness, and mercy.

VERSE

"For the Lord your God is living among you. He is a mighty savior. He will take delight in you with gladness. With His love, He will calm all your fears. He will rejoice over you with joyful songs" (Zephaniah 3:17, NLT).

THREE

Opportunity For Change

IN EARLY 2015, I attempted to plant a fruit and vegetable garden. I say "attempted" because I am not a gardener. I'm quite the opposite. Things that are meant to grow *always* wither and die in my presence. But this time would be different; I was determined to make this garden successful.

I did my research. I consulted my expert gardener friends. I built (or rather had Matt build) the planter box according to the directions. I bought the best dirt. I planted the plants in the right location at just the right distance. I gave them plenty, but not too much, water. And then, I waited. And watched. Even though I followed every rule and did everything right, my plants yielded little fruit. Most of them didn't do anything. I got a few tomatoes and a couple of very large but inedible zucchini. That was it. I was frustrated. *Why didn't my garden grow?* I had done everything right. It didn't make sense.

I've always wanted to live in a world that makes sense. One that is simple, routined, and predictable. One in which I could control every outcome. And in which things were always fair.

As a result, for many years, I gravitated towards the part of God described in Psalm 33 and Isaiah 61, the part that loves justice. That part of God's character made sense to me. So that was the box I put Him in, the way I viewed Him. The problem? Seeing God as a judge didn't help me when my son struggled to speak, while awaiting biopsy results, or even while I wrestled daily to find purpose in a job I no longer loved.

In those moments, I needed a God who was not only just but also loving and compassionate.

But that part of God—the compassionate part—was hard for me to connect with because it was more about Him than me. With *that* God, even though I had done all the right things and followed all the rules, I still experienced pain, and my circumstances didn't always change. Compassion did not look like justice—at least, I didn't understand how it could. It didn't line up with the view of God I had created.

The first words God uses to describe Himself are found in Exodus 34 in His interaction with Moses. At this moment, God is teaching Moses about who He is when He says,

> *The LORD—the LORD is a compassionate and gracious God, slow to anger and abounding in faithful love and truth, maintaining faithful love to a thousand generations, forgiving iniquity, rebellion, and sin (Exodus 34:6-7).*

So, what does it look like for God to be compassionate? It seems like Him loving you, not because He has to, but because He is fond of you as His creation and desires to be in relationship with you. It's Him pursuing you in your suffering. Coming face to face with you. And it's about you letting Him in and allowing Him to rebuild and bring new life, even when it seems like there's nothing left to work with.

Pastor and author Brennan Manning said it this way,

Christianity consists primarily not in what we do for God but in what God does for us—the great, wondrous things that God dreamed up and achieved for us in Christ Jesus. When God comes streaming into our lives in the power of His Word, all He asks is that we be stunned and surprised, let our mouths hang open, and begin to breathe deeply. [1]

One of my favorite illustrations of God's compassion is the story of Hagar in Genesis 16. Hagar is a servant whom Abraham uses to bear a son. During Hagar's pregnancy, she runs away from the home she shares with Abraham and his wife because she is mistreated. But God pursues her and finds her in the wilderness. Hagar is told to return home during this encounter with God's messenger. She is also told that although her son will be the father of many nations, he will live an untamed life— like a wild donkey—and be hostile toward all his relatives. I can't imagine this is the news that Hagar is hoping for. Yet, her response indicates that she had met the God of compassion. It was His presence that brought her comfort. In Genesis 16:13, Hagar says, "You are the God who sees me."

As Christians, we serve a God who sees. When we invite Him, He enters into our suffering with a perspective like no one else because He Himself has suffered.

Because this is true, as Hebrews 12 reminds us, we can study how Jesus did suffering. We can go over His story again and again, looking at all He went through and how He could continue in the mission God had planned for Him. So, how did He do it?

When Jesus' good friend Lazarus died, and Lazarus' sisters mourned their loss, Jesus wept with them. Just before His own death, with full knowledge of what was to come, Jesus gathered His people. He broke bread with them and washed their feet, showing His love for them. Then, amid their fear and confusion, Jesus encouraged his disciples with promises of Heaven and a peace that would only come as a result of His death. He also prayed for us—for you and me—that we would be united and experience the Father's love as He had. Even nearer to His death, Jesus prayed for the forgiveness of those who had nailed Him to the cross.

Jesus lived with the knowledge that He would suffer. He knew His mission. He knew how it would end. Yet, He wondered if there was another way. "If it is possible, let this cup of suffering be taken away from me" (Matthew 26:39, NLT).

Even so, He accepted His role as the Son of Man, as the Messiah, choosing to believe in God's goodness and proclaim His future glory with statements like, "I want Your will to be done, not mine" (Matthew 26:39, NLT), "This is the very reason I came" (John 12:27, NLT), and "Father, I entrust my spirit into your hands" (Luke 23:46, NLT).

Our suffering can bring an opportunity for change because God is in the midst of it. We can encounter Him there. We can be overwhelmed by Him instead of our suffering.

> God does not erase our losses, those empty places in our lives, but He does something almost more miraculous. He fills the loss with the sign of His presence.[2]

Jesus has already been there, and we can learn a lot from studying how He suffered. We can engage and encourage one another through it, which will happen as we allow people into our stories. Through all these things, suffering looks like love... a love that can heal and restore. Not a love that changes or fixes but provides comfort and makes way for rebuilding.

The prospect of rebuilding brings an opportunity for change, but we have to step into it. We must be willing to build into the new instead of rebuilding using an old blueprint or framework.

For most of my adult life, I moved at a pace that left little room for paying attention to things I hadn't planned for. A pace that left me little time to dive into the depths of being *with* God instead of doing *for* Him. I wanted to live well, and I wanted to do what was right. Yet, my inner critic was stifling God's Spirit in me, leading me to scrutinize every action, to measure it against what I thought it looked like to be a successful Christian, a good mom, and a loving wife, all while living a fast-paced existence at work and home.

For most of us, the thoughts and words that run through our minds become what we believe about God, ourselves, and others. My problem was that most days, I felt (and still feel at times) like I was waging war against myself, against the thoughts running through my mind. Thoughts about me, mostly. But also about God.

Your "voices" may not come from an incessant inner critic but a script developed early in your life based on what others spoke into and over you. These unhealthy and unhelpful thoughts that run through your mind may also be based on lies you have been told about yourself, God, or the ones your brain created to protect you from the truth of your circumstances. Some of those voices could have been perpetuated by your culture or the media, leading you to think you are either too much, not enough, or have the ability to do "it" all on your own. We all have voices that attempt to crowd out the voice of God.

In John 4, Jesus meets a Samaritan woman at a well. The woman is unnamed and has come to the well to get water in the heat of the day. No one else is there, and the later text leads me to believe she did this on purpose. The well was a place for gathering, and this woman, in her brokenness, did not want to see or talk with anyone. Jesus meets her at the well with kindness and humility. In John 4:17, the woman shares a statement of vulnerability with Jesus; she says, "I have no husband."

The woman has no husband but has had five previously and presently lives with a man who is not her husband. What does this mean? It means she has likely endured the hurt and grief of being divorced, abandoned, and/or widowed five times. It also means that the certainty of her past, present, and future provision has been taken from her—multiple times. Imagine how she must feel, her daily thoughts about herself, her worth, and her identity. Imagine the voices of the other women in her community.

Jesus' voice rises above it all when He says, "You are right" (v. 17) and "What you have said is true" (v. 18). He didn't say, "What you are thinking is true" or "All of those people whispering about you are right." At that moment, Jesus validated her story and feelings but eliminated the unhealthy and unhelpful voices, lies, and negative thoughts. They were untrue and irrelevant. This interaction with Jesus changed the woman's perspective on herself and her story. She ran into the town, leaving her jar behind. But she also left behind those other voices. How do we know? It's because of what the woman says in John 4:29, as she runs gleefully through town, telling everyone about Jesus: "Come see a man who told me everything I ever did. Could this be the Messiah?"

Do you sense shame in this statement? I don't. Only that Jesus knew her and loved her enough to save her, not only *for* eternity, but *from* all she had been carrying, hiding, and broken by. He didn't change her past, but He allowed her to change her future—and she did!

Paul's letter to the church in Galatia provides us with a way to take advantage of these opportunities for change that God makes available to us:

> Make a careful exploration of who you are and the work
> you have been given, and then sink yourself into that.
> Don't be impressed with yourself. Don't compare your-
> self with others. Each of you must take responsibility
> for doing the creative best you can with your own life
> (Galatians 6:4-5, MSG).

The church in Galatia was struggling because they were listening to the wrong voices, people telling them that to be followers of Christ, they had to follow certain laws and align themselves with a specific identity. This is not what we see in Jesus' interaction with the woman from Samaria, nor what Paul knew was best for the Galatians.

To truly know yourself, you must know and believe the truth about who God is. If He is Creator, you are His creation. If He is love, then you are loved by Him. If He knows and sees all, we are known and seen by Him.

These truths are mysterious and aren't always the easiest to see, especially when the world around us speaks a different language. A language that leads to self-preservation instead of self-awareness. That requires us to work on the outer self, the one that people can see, instead of the inner self, which is our heart and soul.

However, the truth will keep us anchored when all around us continues to change. It will become the secure foundation that takes us out of life's unexpected and unplanned seasons and into rebuilding.

The prophet Amos was called by God away from his life as a shepherd to bring warnings to the northern kingdom of Israel during the time of King Jeroboam II. It was a time of great prosperity for Judah and Israel. Yet, Amos had been called by God to point out the sins of the nation of Israel and proclaim the judgment that would come upon them. Amos' was not an uplifting message of encouragement, yet at its core was God's desire for us to seek Him so that we can live (5:4).

> God sometimes limits us in order to teach us other things... like dependence and rest, and the world is not on my shoulders, it's on His shoulders... and He uses me because He loves me, not because He needs me.[3]

It was in His message from God that Amos provided warnings to the people and put before them an opportunity for dependence, to cry out to their God. This meant that they would have to turn from their evil ways and be completely devoted to and reliant on Him and His vision for them.

To achieve healthy growth and change in our rebuilding, the same is true for us. Psalm 127:1 clarifies that "unless the Lord builds the house, the builders labor in vain." Amos proposed this question: *"Can two walk together without agreeing to meet?"* (Amos 3:3)

For many years I taught social skills to children with autism. One of the skills we worked on was co-regulation. Early in the development of co-regulation comes the challenge of joint attention. I often taught this skill by having the student walk beside me and match my pace. This task required social referencing and joint attention, meaning that the student needed to look at me frequently to ensure they were still walking with me and that their steps and pace aligned with mine. Their task was frequently checking to see where I was and how I was moving so they could match, mimic, react, and adjust their behavior accordingly.

For this skill to be taught, there first had to be an assumption of presence. If the student were unaware of my presence, there would be no referencing or adjusting. This task takes immense concentration. All that's going on internally and externally must be tuned out.

Stepping into the change that comes with rebuilding requires us to slow our pace and lean into the truth of God's presence as our good (Psalm 73:28) as we walk the path God has for us. It is our opportunity to agree to meet with God and walk with Him at His pace in His direction, under His compassionate care.

FINDING HOME IN JERUSALEM

According to Nehemiah 1:3, the people of Israel were "in great trouble and disgrace." They were facing extreme adversity and devastation and were being crushed under the weight of shame. This was not what Nehemiah wanted for his people. It was evident from Nehemiah's prayer that he believed it was not what God desired either.

Nehemiah's burden over the brokenness of the people and their city led him straight to God. Nehemiah lamented the state of God's chosen city and its people and asked God to intervene. Nehemiah began his prayer with praise and recognized God's holiness, power, and faithfulness. He next moved to confession. For Nehemiah, the people's problems became his problems; their sins became his. Nehemiah identified with their brokenness and entered into their pain and need. Then, Nehemiah included a call to remembrance. He asked God to "remember" the instructions He had given Moses and the promise to gather His people and bring them back to the place He had chosen for them to dwell.

Nehemiah knew God had promised to rebuild through these survivors of the exile. Through His power and faithfulness, it would be God who would make way for Nehemiah to get to Jerusalem to continue the process of restoration that had already begun but had been stalled by opposition from the enemies and the despair of the people. Nehemiah emptied himself of his own agenda and made space for God to move and do what only He could.

Knowing that approaching a king in the ancient Near East could be potentially life-threatening[4], Nehemiah moved forward with courage, confidence, and a commitment to God's purpose.

FINDING HOME THROUGH CHANGE

One of my long-time struggles has been with fear. Like most kids, I feared the dark, being alone, heights, and the shadows I saw in my room at night. After an unfortunate incident at the reading table in second grade, I also developed an irrational fear of vomiting.

My most debilitating fear, though, has been my fear of failure. It has a hold on me that I have yet to escape completely. This fear was not preparing me for anything. Instead, it robbed me of trust, worship, joy, and abundance.

As someone who identifies as an Enneagram One, my motivation for all things—truly—is to do what is right, to be right and good. My perspective was that failure was bad. My ability to embrace failure (well, maybe not *embrace* it, but at least accept it as a possibility that did not lead to the end of the world) came as I watched both of my daughters audition for musical theater roles and solos in choir, and as I watched my son step into experiences every day that held the potential for being challenging and uncomfortable.

The Lord gave me the image of holding my son's hand as he got ready to jump into the pool or holding my breath as my daughters' belted the lyrics of yet another audition selection as He whispered, *Do not fear. I will help you. I am holding you, just as you are holding them.*

Alone and seated on my bed, my computer on my lap, I watched as author and speaker Angie Smith told the story of Abraham from Genesis 21. This is the chapter in which God asked Abraham to sacrifice his son, Isaac. Despite his presumed confusion about sacrificing the one through which God had promised to bring many nations, Abraham set out with his son and all he needed to complete the sacrifice.

This was not the first time Abraham had shown his willingness to obey God. We see it first in Genesis 12 when God told

Abraham to leave his family and home and go where God would send him. Even without knowing the specific location, Abraham went. He gave up all that he had known to follow God. The price seemed higher in chapter 21, however. He had been asked to give up something even greater. Angie said it this way, "Abraham had already been asked to give up his past. Now God was asking him to surrender his future."[5]

It was at that point that I began to cry. I was overwhelmed with emotion. Because I knew. I knew what God was asking me to do. He was asking me to decide to surrender my future to Him.

I had grown increasingly unsatisfied with my work as a school psychologist for years. For years, I knew that there was something more that God was calling me to. I didn't know what it was, so I didn't make the big move. It was a change that would remove a large chunk of my family's financial stability, health insurance, and the identity I had been operating under for nearly 20 years. It would require me to give up my past and step into the unknown. To surrender my future.

After a tear-filled conversation with my husband, whose faith has always inspired me (and is one of his spiritual gifts), I let go and stepped into the opportunity for a change I believed God was calling us into. That day, I emailed my boss and asked for an appointment. Later that week, I turned in my resignation letter, which would take effect at the end of that school year. I didn't know what was next, and I was terrified. But I knew it was the right time to make the decision.

For as long as I can remember, I have organized my life by the school year—August to June. First, I was in school; then, I worked *in* the schools. I didn't know life any other way. I didn't have another rhythm.

But August 2016 was different. I wasn't starting anything new. There was no school year to prepare for or district calendars to follow. I felt hollow, directionless, and void of purpose. *Who was I now?*

In anticipation of this transition, a friend suggested that I read Isaiah 43.

The book of Isaiah was written at a time in Israel's history when the nation was experiencing spiritual, cultural, and political unrest. It was written to a people group whose land, lives, and relationship with God were in ruins. The first 39 chapters of the book were written as a call to repentance. Chapters 40 and beyond were written as a call back to God. A call to the hope of deliverance and restoration and to the promise of rebuilding— the type we see in Ezra and Nehemiah.

As I entered a season of uncertainty and unrest, I needed a future hope—not in a job or person or circumstances, but in God alone. I was being called out of ease to a place of need. And God was asking me to come to Him... for my identity, purpose, strength, etc. For my very breath.

God had moved me out of a place where I was comfortable, even if not content—a space where my knowledge was my power. I knew how to do my job, and I did it well. I knew all the rules and helped everyone follow them. I was good there, and despite the heaviness I felt about what the future would look like if I stayed, leaving was much scarier. I didn't know what I would do, and I didn't know how I would make it work.

But that was the thing. It wasn't my job to make it work. It had never been. I had grown so comfortable as the school psychologist that I forgot I needed God there. I could do it on my own. I had had enough faith in myself that faith in Him wasn't required.

There was a day—I don't remember when or where—that God spoke to me about how I had pushed Him away from my job and began defining my identity. I had taken over, forsaking dependence on Him and replacing it with self-reliance. He said: *You don't think you need Me there. I am going to take you where you know you need Me.* The truth was that I needed Him everywhere. I still do. But now I know it.

I need God. You need God. We need God. There has never been a time when we haven't, and there will never be a time when we don't.

One of the great things about God (and there are many) is that He is not limited by the size of our faith or the times when we have misplaced it or pushed it aside. We are the ones who add unnecessary limitations when we don't act in faith.

While our faith doesn't *cause* things to happen, strong belief compels us to act with utter surrender and complete dependence. And, through growing my ability to walk in faith, I have come to believe that dependence on God and freedom are synonymous. We can't experience one without the other.

FINDING HOME IN JERUSALEM

The burden of change in Jerusalem and for its people interrupted Nehemiah's life and took root in his heart.

As cupbearer to the king, Nehemiah lived a life of privilege and had access to the king. Although confident in God and committed to His plan, Nehemiah knew that he would need the king's permission and authority to begin God's mission of rebuilding. He also understood that God ruled over all the kingdoms of the nations (2 Chronicles 20:6).

Nehemiah had spent months in prayer and fasting, was secure in his knowledge of God, and committed to the task he had been called to. He was ready to partner with God in the task of rebuilding Jerusalem.

King Artaxerxes granted Nehemiah's requests and assured him and his group safe passage, protection, and resources on their journey to Jerusalem. Although the king secured the provisions, Nehemiah recognized that his requests had been granted through God's gracious hand, and his needs had been met.

As mentioned earlier, Nehemiah's group was not the first to have returned return to Jerusalem. He would lead the third group of rebuilders. The first two focused on rebuilding the temple and worship systems. The focus of this final group, led by Nehemiah, was to rebuild the city's wall. The walls were important for a couple of reasons: they reestablished the city's boundaries, protected those who resided there, and re-identified the Israelites as God's chosen people. The walls were a sign of identity and belonging for the city and its people.

REBUILDING THROUGH CHANGE

When I was a child, I used to pretend to be asleep to get out of going to church. Mostly because church made me uncomfortable. I was different from the other kids in the class, and they let me know. So, when Sunday morning came, I would stay in bed and keep my eyes shut tight until enough time had passed and it was too late to go to church. It didn't always work. But it worked enough times to keep me trying it again and again. At least, that's how I remember it.

This is what I was like in those years when I was overwhelmed with postpartum depression and its aftermath. I remained in my figurative bed, with my eyes shut tight as God tried to wake me, to draw me to Him. I resisted His efforts because I knew that I would have to change if I began to trust Him again. Even though it was painful and destructive, I was comfortable in my misery.

So, I pretended to sleep. Made excuses and created questions and doubts. Fortunately, He didn't give up. He continued to pursue me until I woke up. Until I looked Him in the eye and said, *I believe You. I trust You.*

That's how it began, with acknowledging Him once again. By removing the veil that had kept Him blurry and me aloof, I could see Him, and I knew He could see me. I was still afraid, but my eyes had been opened.

Then later, He opened my ears to His voice. With His still, small voice and each of my small steps, I began to come back to life.

Looking back, I can see many brave moments—a first conversation, the first time I hit publish or delete. The times I said yes and the times when I said no. They were all brave because I had felt scared before each of them. Yet, moment by moment, step by step, my heart began to soften. And, as my heart became pliable, God changed its desires. My desires.

When I heard His voice, and when I hear it now, the only possible response is obedience. He keeps saying, *"This is the way; walk in it"* (Isaiah 30:21). And, I walk. Not because my fear is gone. But because He is God and He is with me, I am braver than I know.

Change is possible. You can change. You are braver than you know.

Breathe

DEFINITION

To draw air into and expel it from the lungs; to inhale and exhale freely.

A DEEPER LOOK

It is God's breath that brings life. By His breath, He formed the earth and filled it with its inhabitants. Breathing is a rhythm of taking in God's abundance and taking notice of His presence and power through His Spirit, and then releasing all that has been keeping you from experiencing freedom. God desires to breathe life into the soul that is in need.

VERSE

"Then David said to his son Solomon, 'Be strong and courageous, and do the work. Don't be afraid or discouraged, for the Lord God, my God, is with you. He won't leave you or abandon you until all the work for the service of the Lord's house is finished'" (1 Chronicles 28:20, CSB).

FOUR

Evaluate The Rubble

WHO AM I? I thought as I stared into the mirror. It was the first day of work for most of my former colleagues. But instead of heading out the door to work, I stood in my bathroom, in my pajamas, staring at my reflection. Outwardly, I looked the same. On the inside, though, I was different.

I'd held the same professional position for 17 years. It was the one that I had trained for and was good at. I had worked inside my comfort zone for years, and God was asking me to break out and go deeper. God was building new passions and gifts within me. Much of what I thought I knew about myself and my life had changed. God was breathing newness into me and writing a different story for my life. I didn't know the main character very well.

I've always been a deep thinker, not one who understands the purpose of small talk or appreciates superficial social interaction. However, as an extreme introvert, I often kept my deep thoughts to myself because they frequently made people uncomfortable and left me misunderstood. Yet, this was how God asked me to connect with people, first with anonymity behind a computer screen and then as a writer, teacher, and women's ministry leader. I was the one who could get children to open up or feel comfortable in new or strange situations. But God was asking me to connect to women in ways I didn't understand, wasn't comfortable with, and wasn't always well-received. How was I supposed to do this? I didn't know how. I wasn't good at it.

What I had done with my life previously, as a professional and a follower of Christ, had only scratched the surface of God's abundance. I had not devoured God's Word at its discovery (Jeremiah 15:16). I had taken just enough of God to get by, to create a life that left me feeling capable and self-sufficient. Until it wasn't enough anymore. I was afraid to go deeper because deeper was uncomfortable. Staying comfortable was not an option, though, because I missed my need for God there.

Although there can be great hurt and pain in the deep, there is also great power. To go deep is to enter into vulnerability with God and others. We need *deep* to connect with God. We need deep to understand the compassion of Jesus. We need deep to experience the Holy Spirit in His fullness.

As we breathe deep, we are transformed. It's in the depths that we can connect with God and begin to understand who we are.

One of the hardest parts of rebuilding is intentionally taking time to go through the rubble. These are the parts of your life that didn't go as planned. The pieces of the people, places, and relationships that have been broken. The wounds that are buried deep inside.

If there's one thing I've heard repeatedly from the women I've coached, counseled, and taught over the years is their obsession with escaping their past. The parts of their stories that have already happened, especially those that have been challenging or caused pain. These are the things they often struggle to understand and desperately want to change.

Statements and questions that begin with *if only* or *why* are the hardest to answer because the reason for suffering and brokenness, although simple, does not necessarily give us warm-fuzzy feelings or help our desire for a re-do disappear. The reason is sin. It has been around since the beginning of time, and as long as we live in this world, we will experience the effects of sin—our own, the sins of others, and the sins of the world.

Genesis 1-2 describes how God created order from chaos by forming and filling the earth with light and darkness, plants, animals, and people. In its initial state, God saw all that He had created and called it good. Except for people who were created in His image, stamped with His imprint, and brought to life with His breath—only them He called *very good*.

In Genesis 3, we are introduced to temptation, doubt, and sin. Eve was tempted, listened to a voice other than God's, and Adam followed her lead. Then, following their sin, Adam and Eve recognized their mistake and hid from God. They didn't understand that God was not the one they needed to hide from; He was their hiding place, the only one who could keep them safe—because their relationship with their Creator secured their identity.[1] His was the only voice they needed to listen to because they could trust Him.

Instead of moving away from God, we can run *to* Him for safety in times of trouble.

The sin of man was not a part of God's original design or definition of order, but He wasn't surprised by it either. He was ready with a plan to save His people. Similarly, God has not been surprised by anything in your story; He has never left you alone. You're not being punished, and you have not been forgotten.

God is not in the business of changing our pasts, but He does provide the freedom to move toward a new future. God's presence and power will allow you to experience healing and hope and provide the courage you need to take up the work of rebuilding, including what is often the hardest part—evaluating the rubble.

The word *rebuild* means to build something again after it has been damaged or injured, to make it like new without completely replacing it. I like this synonym for rebuild: "to put in good order." When brokenness is a part of our story, our lives are disrupted, and things feel out of order. This is when rebuilding becomes necessary.

Our brokenness can look like many things: legal issues, relationship struggles, betrayal, trauma, church hurt, illness, etc. I have seen this in my life as I've learned what it looks like to rebuild as someone with chronic health issues.

In the summer of 2018, severe migraines, unexplained pain, and fatigue turned my life upside down. As I've made my way toward healing over the past several years, I've had to evaluate who I can be in this new season. I had to answer the questions: *What is at stake if I allow this to win? What is at stake if I don't rebuild?*

I have been changed in this process, even though so much of my identity remains the same.

FINDING HOME IN JERUSALEM

With safe passage and provisions secured, Nehemiah made his way to Jerusalem. After traveling for approximately two months, he arrived in the city and... got right to work? No. He waited three days. Why? Was he resting? Was he waiting for God to provide further instruction? The text does not say. All we know is that Nehemiah allowed three days to pass before he set out to evaluate the current state of the city and its wall.

From earlier in the book, we know that Nehemiah had great faith in his God. A faith that had not been put off as he waited four months in prayer before approaching the king about his need for time away. Then, after his long journey, Nehemiah waits once again.

Have you ever experienced a season of waiting?

Depending on its length, waiting can make you feel like a tree in winter. Barren. Empty. Lifeless. Yet, I can assure you, so much is happening that you can't see. Underneath, the soil protects the roots of trees, keeping them warm and nourished. Their bare branches allow you to see what needs to be pruned or reshaped. There is rest and replenishment: refashioning and removal.

Rebuilding sometimes looks like waiting, being still, and resting in preparation for the work that is to come. It is taking time to shed broken thoughts and relationships. The between is the space in the middle of the promise and the fulfillment, faith, and sight. It is where hope is born, and we make a decision.

You are free to wait. You have permission to experience peace, even when the dark days continue longer than expected. In the winter, the evidence of growth is unseen but is still important. So it is with us. While we wait, we have the time to rest and reevaluate. To cultivate the deeper truths of ourselves and God.

Waiting is an important part of the process of growth. In the future, the fruit will come. Our choices are acting as if the promise is true or fearing it will never come. We can take our cues from Nehemiah or continue to wonder how rebuilding will be possible.

Although you may not know when or how, the time for rebuilding will come. God has promised it.

Before gathering a crew of builders and sharing with them the burden for rebuilding God had put into his heart, Nehemiah took a ride through the city of Jerusalem.

Nehemiah evaluated the state of the wall as he made his way through the city's brokenness, destruction, and emptiness. He did the hard work of navigating through the rubble and squeezing through the narrow spaces to determine what remained that could be used and what was too damaged to serve

Israel in the rebuilding process. As Nehemiah led the remnant people to rebuild their city, he also sought to discover which parts of the wall remained.

The problem of brokenness was big, and he wasn't clear on the plan's specifics. Still, Nehemiah knew what God had promised and that nothing had ever been too broken for God to rebuild. A quote attributed to Mother Teresa goes like this:

> I've never had clarity, but I've always had trust. So I will pray that you trust God.

In the absence of clarity, Nehemiah had trust. And that was enough.

Nehemiah also knew that it was impossible to rebuild something new if you don't know where you're starting from. In order to rebuild, a remnant was required. After all, the people of Israel weren't starting over with nothing. They were continuing a process that God had begun many generations prior. Their home had been secured for them before they were even born. It would be impossible for them to find it again if they didn't know where it had been.

FINDING HOME THROUGH THE RUBBLE

I spent much of my life believing that being different was wrong, not for others but for myself. It was a lie that grew and, at times, consumed me. But it was more than that.

It was the spring of 2017, and I was teaching a Bible study I had written on the book of Acts to a group of women in my church. It was my birthday week, and I was preparing to teach on the Acts 13-18 text. One verse God revealed to me during my teaching preparation was 2 Corinthians 3:3:

You show that you are a letter from Christ... written not
with ink but with the Spirit of the living God.

My life was a message? God was revealing Himself through me? I
believed this for the women I was teaching, but as I read that
verse, I didn't believe it for myself.

That's when God spoke to my doubt: *"Stop apologizing for the
way I created you."*

I had been calling something "bad" that God had called
"good." I had been dismissing what I knew about Him and
whom He had created me to be. I confessed my disbelief to God
and to the women that week. I turned 42 believing that God
loved me.

Yet, less than a month later, I woke up feeling empty. There
was a heaviness to my heart and my body. Immediately upon
waking, I felt like I had nothing left to give. I didn't understand
how to give from that place. How to be light when everything
around me felt so dark. How to cry out to God and be filled and
refilled when feeling different felt wrong.

As we attempt to move beyond our seasons of struggle or hardship, our first task is to evaluate the ruin. We have to know what's
broken to fix it. We see Nehemiah do this as he rides through the
city alone. He takes an inventory of the brokenness. He wants to see
what's left that can still be useful and what needs to be removed.
We see him evaluate each part of the city, its wall, and gates.

Understanding my own story and how it has brought me to
this point has been crucial to moving forward in my mission of
rebuilding. In my most recent evaluation, I discovered that God
has always called me toward transformation and home. By
moving me from the dark basements of life to places of light, He
has helped me see who He has created me to be and how I can
be used to help others rebuild as well.

Has it been hard? Yes! But it's been necessary.

We don't want to rebuild on top of ashes or destruction with faulty wiring or broken beams. We need to know the tools to use as we rebuild and move toward healing.

Our brokenness can look like grief, trauma, health crises, relationship struggles, etc. What worked for us while we tried to survive hardship or trauma may not work for us as we rebuild. We need to know that before we even begin. We may need new boundaries or to resurrect old ones—boundaries that were forgotten during our struggle.

Think about your own most recent season of hardship or struggle. What has been left behind in its wake? What, if anything, will serve you as you move forward and rebuild? Or, think about a time when you were encouraged to "move on" without assessing the damage. What was the result? You likely still felt brokenness on the inside, whether it appeared that way on the outside or not.

As we look through the Bible, we can see that it is filled with the theme of God's love for the poor, broken, lonely, and oppressed. Psalm 34:18 says,

> The Lord is near the brokenhearted; He saves those
> crushed in Spirit.

This psalm was written by King David, who, prior to its writing, had been the target of hatred and harassment, had experienced brokenness and loneliness, and—as evidenced by this psalm and others—also knew what it felt like for God to be near and to make way for rebuilding.

Sometimes, to recover what's been lost, we have to return to where we lost it. To the beginning, to see what went wrong.

The book of Genesis says that in the beginning, God spoke, and it was so. He said it, and it happened. All of it, by His word and His breath.

"Did God really say?" That was the question that led to the

first sin. The question that caused Adam and Eve to wonder if there was something more, if God was holding out on them.

Returning to the beginning, we can discover what has been lost and why. But when you get there, you may find that what you're missing hasn't been lost. Maybe it's been forgotten or covered by lies or doubt. Perhaps you've stopped agreeing with what you once knew to be true.

Before the serpent spoke a question to Eve, God had already spoken over her. After creating man and woman in His own image, Genesis 1:31 says that "God saw all that He had made, and it was very good."

> Being made in God's image and reflecting His likeness is the truest thing about you.[2]

Knowing this about yourself is essential; it is the place to start.

Self-awareness is the beginning of change. Knowing what God has already said about you and to you is part of self-awareness. After all, if you don't know where you are, how can you figure out where you need to go?

Only by first saying, "I am here," can we begin to say, *"Here I am, Lord."*

FINDING HOME IN JERUSALEM

After surveying the damage, Nehemiah gathered the people who would be part of rebuilding the wall. The evaluation was complete, and it was time to decide and get started. Although Nehemiah had chosen to leave his job as the king of Persia's cupbearer for some time to partner with God in this rebuild, the *people* still needed to decide. Would they willingly partner in this mission?

In Nehemiah 2:17-18, Nehemiah makes his plea to the

people. He called them to action, not just for the sake of their city but to come out from under the weight of shame and the contempt of their enemies. This rebuild was not just about their present but also their past and future.

Taking the first step of rebuilding is often the hardest, but it is the most important. Remember that the first step doesn't have the be the biggest or get you the furthest. You can take one step at a time, knowing that God has promised to rebuild and will continue to make a way as you move forward.

God made way for the rebuilding of His city and His people. Nehemiah confirms this in 2:18 when after agreeing to rebuild their city, God strengthened the hands of His people, and they trusted that He would provide for them as they rebuilt. God will make way for you too.

In the wake of crisis, trauma, and adversity, we are often left with a mess to clean up. The debris in our hearts and minds leaves us with shame, threatening our emotional stability and ability or desire to connect with ourselves and others. The wreckage that exists on the outside can brand us as broken and insecure, leaving us vulnerable to criticism and additional hardship.

The mess of shame, insecurity, and continued brokenness can only be removed by God. Nehemiah knew this and responded accordingly at the first sign of opposition.

For the rebuilders in Jerusalem, adversity came immediately after they committed to the mission of rebuilding. Their decision to move toward healing and God's promise of abundance led to opposition from their enemies—those who didn't want to see them prosper or think they deserved it.

Nehemiah responded to this opposition with a statement of truth, clearly stating his belief in God's purpose for the group of rebuilders and confidence that God would grant them their success.

One continual and unavoidable part of the rebuilding process for the nation of Israel was opposition. Their adversaries challenged them frequently as they repeatedly came against Nehemiah and the people with mocking, taunting, threats of violence, etc. The enemies were against the mission because rebuilding the walls would make Israel a stronger nation; they would be less vulnerable to attack and could not easily take on the culture and customs of those around them.

Over and over, Nehemiah responded to this opposition by returning to God's promises and His help. We must do the same! The people of Israel, led by Nehemiah, were partnering with God, which meant trusting God to do His part and continuing to walk in obedience, even if that included fighting against the opposition as they rebuilt.

REBUILDING THROUGH THE RUBBLE

Remember the garden I had carefully planned and planted in 2015? The one that had been perfect in every way, except that it had yielded no fruit?

In early spring 2016, I was out in the yard, cleaning up all of the dead foliage from the winter, and I decided to clear up the would-be fruit and vegetable garden. It had been months since I had looked at it. The last I had seen, all was lost. Do you know what I found when I cleared all that was dead? The grapevine, the one thing planted outside my perfect planter box, had resurrected itself. Somehow. Someway. There was new life there. And I hadn't done a thing.

That's what Jesus does for us. He brings new life. Even when it doesn't make sense or seems impossible. So, whether you're meeting Him for the first time, are getting reacquainted with Him after some time away, or have known Him your whole life, He has something for you. Jesus is the way. He is our way out of sin. He is our way *through* suffering.

In Isaiah 43, the prophet Isaiah speaks to God's people about their restoration. The time beyond their seasons of struggle and brokenness when He will make way for rebuilding. In verses 18-19, Isaiah says,

> *Do not remember the past events, pay no attention to the*
> *things of old. Look, I am about to do something new;*
> *even now, it is coming. Do you not see it?*

Rebuilding into the new requires evaluating the rubble and leaving it in the past. This allows us to discover our new starting point without taking the baggage and burden into our new home. It's time to stop identifying yourself by your season of struggle and move forward toward rebuilding. Do you see it?

Deep

DEFINITION

Extending far from some surface or area; difficult to penetrate or comprehend.

A DEEPER LOOK

There is depth to our brokenness. Yet, there is a greater depth to God's abundant grace. To know God means more than just knowing *about* Him. It means having a steady, habitual, and active relationship *with* Him. To experience the depth of who He is and who He has created us to be.

VERSE

"But you are a chosen people, a royal priesthood, a holy nation, God's special possession, that you may declare the praises of Him who called you out of darkness into His wonderful light" (1 Peter 2:9).

FIVE

Rebuilding In Community

I CAN'T REMEMBER a time when podcasts weren't a thing. Can you? They became a lifeline to me when migraines became my norm, and my need for input and learning wasn't easily or enjoyably found in books anymore. I still listen to podcasts while I exercise, put puzzles together, prepare meals, etc. But not as much as I used to.

One of the first podcasts I listened to was *The Happy Hour* by Jamie Ivey. There was an episode in June 2016 in which the guest talked about a specific type of prayer; she called it Healing Prayer. The kind in which you ask questions like: "God, where were you when _____? What were you doing? What were you feeling?"[1]

As I listened to the women talking about this type of intentional prayer, I knew where God was asking me to go—to my son's first years of life. It was a time I hadn't thought of in years, but at that moment, I could feel the pain of the wound that remained deep within me. It felt fresh.

So, I asked Him, *"God, where were You during that time? What were You doing? What were You feeling?"*

He responded, *"I was there. I walked the halls with you. I cried with you. My heart broke for you. I grieved for your losses and celebrated the victories that were to come. I sat beside you and whispered the right questions into your ears. I strengthened you when you didn't think you could go on. I was always there, even when you didn't want to talk to me."*

It brought me to tears (much like it's doing now as I type this). To know that God was so kind to me, even when I rejected Him. When I wrestled and fought to believe. Why would He do that? The simple answer: love.

There is a depth to God's love that is beyond our comprehension. In 1 John 3:1, John writes,

> *See what great love the Father has lavished on us, that we should be called children of God! And that is what we are!*

Beloved is the identity that God wants us to take hold of. To live lives marked by His love, to carry His love with us—to whoever and in whatever manner He brings before us. We can love only because He first loved us (1 John 4:19).

My intellect has always been both my superpower and my kryptonite (you know, the only thing that was able to weaken Superman's powers).

I have loved learning, intellectual activity, and acquiring information for as long as I can remember. Because this is not true of everyone, I've often felt uncomfortable in social spaces due to sideways glances or confused expressions that reveal what others are probably thinking about me: *That's strange* or *I don't get it.* It may not surprise you then that the lie that crept into my thoughts was: *This is the wrong way to be.*

That's why it was so confusing when God began taking away my passion for working with children, particularly students with autism, to connecting and engaging with women. It was in 2017 that my mission became: *Inspiring others to discover their value and purpose in Christ—leading them to a belief that God is alive and active and helping them connect their needs to His transforming power.*

This new mission and my story with God's words led me in 2017 to the word *deep*. Although I had been learning more about God, I hadn't yet explored His depths. One of the verses I discovered that year was 1 Corinthians 2:10 (MSG):

> *The Spirit, not content to flit around on the surface, dives*
> *into the depths of God, and brings out what God*
> *planned all along.*

It made me realize that if the Spirit was in me, I could do this too.

In spaces (at least in the ones I've found myself) where the Bible and faith are the primary topic of conversation, the teachings and discussions around "self"-anything are minimal. And, most often, when the "self" is talked about, it's negative. When Jesus called His disciples, saying, "Whoever wants to be my disciple must deny themselves and take up their cross and follow me" (Matthew 16:24), I don't believe that He meant "everything you are and everything you desire is bad."

It was more like, "How you understand yourself has been confused by many things. Follow me, and you will understand yourself the ways I intended you to. I want you to know through abiding with me the way my Father created you to be."

Knowing self from this perspective can change everything! We were all created with unique strengths given to us by our Creator. These strengths can be downplayed, misused, or even forgotten throughout our lives. My challenge to you is this: Consult your Creator and ask, *Whom have you created me to be? Where have I got this wrong? Help me make it right by Your standards, not by mine.* This consultation allows us to free ourselves from the hold that insecurity, doubt, and comparison have on us by looking to the One who knit us together at the start and who wants good, abundant life for us now and at the end.

The word for him/herself used in Matthew 16:24 is *heautou,* a pronoun used to distinguish one person from another or a group of persons from another. It is not a word used for the soul—*psuché*—which describes our very breath, the center and essence of who we are as creatures made in the image and imitating the living God.

My story in 2016 took me to my very breath. In 2017, I learned how to breathe deeply. The more I dove into the depths of God, the more I learned about myself. I discovered that God created me with the desire to learn, grow, and use my mind as designed. These are my strengths, not my weaknesses.

Once I began embracing who God created me to be, I discovered how beautiful it was to love God with my mind and to have a thinking faith. Digging deep into His Word with intense inquiry doesn't detract from who He is. In fact, it gave me a deeper knowledge and a more accurate picture of who He is.

I have felt like both the smartest person in the room and like I know nothing. Both too old and too young. Too much and not enough. I have feared failure and also success. I have wondered if things were moving too fast or too slow. I've kept silent and spoken out.

I have felt all these things, sometimes all at once. But none of them define me. God has defined me and set my heights and depths. He has allowed these things to be a part of my story.

My family and I have enjoyed watching each movie in the *Toy Story* franchise. Although *Toy Story 4* is not my favorite of the group, there was one quote I wrote down while watching it.

In the movie, the Bo Peep character has a central role. While she had been a part of the *Toy Story* cast of characters all along, it is in the fourth movie that she returns with a larger part to play in the narrative. After being separated from the other toys, Bo is reunited with Woody and joins him in a toy rescue mission.

Along the way, Bo introduces Woody to the toys she has met while apart. One of the toys Woody meets is Duke Kaboom, a motorcycle stunt action figure. Woody and Bo need Duke to help them in their mission, but their request triggers Duke's memory of the brokenness in his own story and the lie that has crept in since; because of this memory, he refuses to help them. Bo's words of encouragement to Duke are, "Be [the Duke] who you are right now."[2]

What can we learn from Bo Peep's words of wisdom? Our stories of brokenness—while they don't define us—are a part of who we are. Our stories make us unique, distinct individuals who make up the diversity in the kingdom of God.

As you progress in rebuilding, you will need others, and others will need you—your gifts, strengths, quirks, scars from old wounds, and lessons you've learned. These are evidence of God's creativity in the creation He called good. We can't be like everyone else, so let's not try.

Be authentically you. You are needed.

FINDING HOME IN JERUSALEM

Have you ever wondered why it was Nehemiah that God chose to lead the task of rebuilding? After all, even though he was an Israelite, he had chosen not to return to Jerusalem but to remain in service to the Persian empire. After the wall was built, Nehemiah returned to Susa, leaving the Jewish people to live out their days under new leadership. Was he the right choice?

Nehemiah's name means "the Lord has comforted."[3] He lives into his name by presenting the reader with an example of a leader who not only led a physical rebuilding effort but also brought hope and safety to a broken people. By responding to a burden and taking care of the assignment God had called him to, Nehemiah also led the people toward God and community and equipped them to fight against opposition and for their future.

Throughout the book, Nehemiah recognizes the constant presence of God as he often moves seamlessly between interaction with others and conversation with God. This sacred transition appears first in Nehemiah 2:4. Between the king's asking for information regarding Nehemiah's request and Nehemiah's response to the king, the text says, "So I prayed to the God of the heavens...." Right in the middle of his fear and emotional burden, Nehemiah prays. He calls out to God, and his prayers are answered as evidenced by the following verses.

Nehemiah's ability to slip without hesitation into prayer occurs again in Nehemiah 4:4-5, 5:19, 6:14, and 13:31. His access to God was not limited by his location, environment, or circumstances. As an Israelite, Nehemiah had heard the stories of generations prior, of God's presence with His people. He also knew the stories of the days before the exile and what it was like to maintain his faith, even while living outside of Jerusalem. Nehemiah believed God and understood the significance of the Jewish people returning to Jerusalem in the present and what it could mean for their future.

Nehemiah experienced what it was like to make God his home. He was like no one else in his time. That was a good thing!

REBUILDING THROUGH COMMUNITY

I became someone different in 2014—the year of *empty*.

After standing on that stage in January—the one I had almost left behind because of my fear—I was changed. I was the same, but I was different.

Then came the rainy Saturday in February. I sat in front of the computer screen with my eyes wide and my heart filled. I was alone in the room but didn't feel alone anymore. The vision

I had before that day was me alone on a crazy train headed nowhere and fast. As the rain fell outside my window, I finally felt like I was no longer the only one.

It was a spur-of-the-moment decision to sign up to watch the IF: Gathering in the winter of 2014. Matt had been sick in bed for a few days, and I was desperate for time to myself. *What is this IF: Gathering?* I didn't know nor anyone else because it was its first year in existence. It was the day of the event, and it was free. *Why not?*

My soul was stirred at its depths as I watched women share the word of God to encourage women all over the globe to respond to the question, *If God is real, how will you respond?*

I didn't have an answer to that question... yet. But for the first time in a long time, I felt seen. I wasn't the only one God was asking to make their faith real and move toward new spaces and people groups. I wasn't the only one who wasn't satisfied with the status quo, who wanted more for my life and longed to live on mission and with purpose. Finally, I'd found women who were like me. Women who wanted to know God, not just about Him; they wanted to know Him by experience. They were hearing from God and doing something about it. I felt like I belonged once again.

This was me now. Probably who I'd always been, but I'd been afraid to even think about what wanting *more* meant.

From that point on, I began reading more and listening to Christian women speakers, searching for answers to what was happening to me and hoping to find out that it was happening to someone else, somewhere else. The more I read and listened, the more amazed I was. Even without personal knowledge of me, these women seemed to understand me and how I felt.

At that time, I didn't know many people in my real life who were speaking my language. It was a language of the Holy Spirit. Of desire. Of burden. Of purpose.

I wanted to be used by God, and it felt strange. Not because I didn't think it was right, but because I didn't know many people at that time who understood that. Yes, I knew people who also wanted to be used by God. But I didn't know too many filled with as much urgency and passion for it as I was. Who had a hunger and thirst for the opportunity. Who feared they might miss it if they didn't act NOW. I didn't know how much I needed them until they started appearing on my computer screen, one by one.

I wanted more, and God was giving it to me. First, He gave me the desire to seek Him, be immersed in His Word, learn, and grow. It was like a craving I couldn't satisfy—the desire to know Him more. I couldn't imagine living in a state where I was not seeking Him. To be out of His presence and in a state of ingratitude or indifference felt wrong.

A necessary part of seeking to be filled by God's Spirit was first becoming empty before Him. This meant I had to set aside my agenda and expectations and be open to whatever God had for me. It meant a new posture for prayer and worship—using open hands to symbolize release and a means to receive. It meant making myself less and allowing Him to become greater.

As I approached God with a new posture of the body and heart, I began to understand what it meant to live for Jesus. To live as one loved and rescued by Him and free to follow Him with confidence and expectancy. Prior to this journey, which God began in April 2012, I was mostly neutral, medium, status quo. I knew Jesus but was not always passionate about Him. I was familiar with God and the Bible and church; they were a part of my life, but I had not lived for them.

I was a mediocre Christian, with moments of spark and moderate intensity. I wasn't all in, especially when life was hard. When things got tough, I wanted to quit or strive to create my own alternate story without stopping to ask God what He wanted. I wasn't free.

That Saturday in February 2014, God brought me home to

the idea that freedom is only possible when you're willing to give up everything and say yes to anything.

Rebuilding requires community—a community whose foundation is in God himself.

We were created to be in relationship—with God and each other. We were designed to be connected; "It is not good" for us to be alone (Genesis 2:18). However, many of our life experiences, struggles, crises, and trauma have the potential to disrupt connection.

These disruptions can leave us vulnerable to criticism, with a tendency toward comparison, subject to the control of others, and uncertain of ourselves and those around us.

When the opportunity to rebuild comes around, we can put the broken pieces together or build a team of safe and emotionally healthy people who can join us in our rescue mission. Those who will pray for our growth and good, counsel and encourage us, and stand alongside us as we rebuild. Just as the people of Israel joined together for their common good.

God has already said who we are. He has set us in our places and with our people for a purpose. Are you, am I, brave enough to believe Him? Each choice we make today—even the choice to make space to hear the voice of God—will impact the future, both yours and those around you.

Rebuilding in community is about so much more than the value it brings to the present. It is a commitment to a better future, which could be days, months, or even years away.

After God freed the nation of Israel from slavery and oppression, He planned to take them to a land of abundance where they could worship Him freely. He would be their God, and they would be His people. However, because they allowed fear to overcome their growing faith in their God, the Israelites spent more than 40 years wandering in the desert.

Despite their unfaithfulness, God continued to provide. Each day, manna appeared for them to collect, cook, and consume.

The challenge? Only collect enough for one day. Don't take more than you need, and don't save any overnight. There would always be enough, and always there the next day.

But because some of the people of Israel were still learning to trust God, they collected too much and found that it was inedible. Exodus 16:20 (CSB) says, "Some of the people left part of it until morning, and it bred worms and stank." Can you imagine?

What has God provided you today? Are you trying to live on yesterday's provision? Take what and who God has given you today and get to work. Believe in *Him* for tomorrow.

HAVE you ever been on an amazing vacation? One that blew all of your expectations out of the water? When Matt and I took the kids to Disneyland at the end of June 2018, that's what I experienced.

It had been years since we had braved the land of Disney as a family of five. Honestly, I had been avoiding it. Our previous experience had been good, but navigating the needs of three kids, including one who was very particular about, well… everything, had been exhausting. Not a real vacation for me.

But our 2018 experience was different. It was magical and felt like a miracle!

The photos from our time in Disneyland are a marker for me. They mark the point in my life narrative when the plot twisted (once again) in a new direction. What had once seemed like they were in the background of the storyline—the sometimes annoying but fairly insignificant plot points—came to the foreground. It was all I could see, and I wondered why I had ignored it for so long.

I came down from the high of our Disney adventure and fell into a deep, dark valley. July 2018 was the month when I experienced intense pain for more than half of its days. My quality of life took a drastic turn that month; I could barely get out of bed, and tasks that I once viewed as routine and simple became extraordinarily challenging and complex. It wasn't just the pain getting to me but the absence of hope.

While I had been experiencing similar symptoms since 2014, they had been nothing compared to July 2018. This month was a pivot point for me. This wasn't normal, and I could no longer handle it alone. My crisis response kicked in, and instead of running toward God, I ran toward medical intervention. I wanted answers and a way to fix all that had derailed my life. Only after the answers didn't satisfy and the remedies stopped working did I cry out to God for healing.

I was disappointed when the healing didn't come. I knew God could heal me, so why didn't He? It wasn't until later that year that I discovered the reason why.

I lay in bed... awake. I saw midnight, 1, 2, and 3 am. Each time I thought to myself, I have 4, 3, 2, and 1 hour(s) for this headache to go away. I just wanted to sleep. I prayed for God to take my pain away. This was just what I had feared would happen.

It was October 31, 2018—the night before I was set to leave for Minneapolis to attend Ezer Collective.

I had hesitated to register. It would be my first-ever solo air travel, and I had yet to find any remedy for my chronic migraines. I believed God was prompting me to join other women leaders in this amazing opportunity. But I was also unbelievably afraid. *How would my body handle the flight? Would I be able to navigate the airports on my own? I believe, Lord, help me with my unbelief (Mark 9:24).*

At the end of August, one of the doctors I had seen asked me to keep track of my migraines to rate them on a 1-10 scale. In the two months since I had developed a good idea of my functioning level based on my pain ratings. With a migraine at the 1-

4 level, the pain was annoying but bearable; I could still handle my normal activity at a slower pace and for a shorter time. A rating of 5-7 was more challenging; the pain made concentrating difficult, lights and sounds were "offensive," and social interaction was challenging. Still, I could push through if something needed to be done. On those 8-10 days, my pain and fatigue were intense—and not just in my head, but in my entire body— and I spent most of these days in bed, in the dark, as my senses were heightened to an overwhelming level.

The night before Ezer, my pain was at 7+, and I couldn't sleep, which I knew would worsen the pain and my anxiety about the trip. I never did get any sleep that night, and my prayers went unanswered. As I navigated the airport, my anxiety and pain increased. I did not want to feel this way the entire trip. What a waste it would be!

I would love to say that the pain eventually went away. That God answered my prayers. But that's not what happened. Instead, I spent the two days of the conference moving between 8-10 on the pain scale. I sat through all the speakers and workshops but wasn't even sure my notes would be coherent. I skipped all social activities and spent much of my free time alone in my bed at the Airbnb.

Was it even worth it? At the time, I was miserable, and it all seemed so senseless.

During the conference's final session, the entire group of women was taken through an activity in which we were given space to ask God two questions: "What are you asking me to say goodbye to?" and "What are you asking me to say hello to?"

I felt God's presence, and His answer stronger than I had the entire trip. *Say goodbye to asking for healing and for Me to make it easier, and say hello to asking for help.*

As soon as I started asking God to heal me, I knew He *could*. Yet, He hadn't. So, I took matters into my own hands. I pursued healing with all I had—energy, money, passion, etc. The truth was: health had become my idol. Healing had become my god. I wanted to heal more than anything else, and God was asking me to let it go. To take that option off the table.

My sin had not caused my suffering, but my suffering had caused me to sin. It had shifted my loyalty and the focus of my longing to something I could see and feel rather than toward the God who was unseen. I didn't believe that He was good and loving or that I belonged to Him because He wasn't what I longed for.

Later, when I told people about my experience at Ezer, they often wondered aloud whether I had heard God correctly. They said, "Maybe it's not a *no*, just a *not yet*." Maybe, but I didn't think so. And I still haven't found that to be true over five years later.

Can God still heal me? Of course, He can. But I believe He wants me to ask for help instead. Help from Him, from my family and friends, from my community. Is help better than healing? Most days, it is, but there are some days when I find the idol of health trying to push its way back in.

What help versus healing has done is forced me to embrace my limits and reach out to God and others when I need it. It has allowed me to slow down and pay attention to the needs of my mind and body. I can see now that even though it's not what I wanted, it's what I needed. And probably still need.

FINDING HOME IN JERUSALEM

Nehemiah 3 takes the reader on a journey around the boundaries of the city of Jerusalem, beginning at the north wall and going down along the west wall to the south wall and up the east side. Each section of the text includes a list of individuals from all over the region who came together to rebuild the doors and gates, making the wall even more secure.

I will admit that the repetitive nature of the list of names,

gates, doors, locks, etc., is difficult to read, and at times I have
been tempted to skip it altogether. However, the people and
places were included for a specific purpose. This list tells us that
this group was socially and economically diverse, each holding
their own story of the exile and return to Jerusalem. None were
expert builders. Each one rebuilt sections of the wall and gates
next to and beside each other, doing their part and using their
specific gifts, each one essential to achieving the ultimate goal of
rebuilding the wall and securing the city of Jerusalem.

Another important thing to note about this portion of the
narration is that it summarizes the entire build from start to
finish. Nehemiah 3 offers hope to the reader, confirming that
the wall *will be* completed despite the opposition that continues
to come against the people in chapters 4-7. This is a great
encouragement for our own seasons of rebuilding!

The word *repair* (*chazaq*) occurs 35 times in Nehemiah 3.
Chazaq means to *make strong and firm* (citation). This rebuild was
not a quick fix or a temporary patch that would get the people
by until the *real* repair could be done; this rebuild was meant to
last.

The wall and gates in Jerusalem weren't just about the
present Israelite community. They were also intended to set up
the city and its people for a better future. For many generations,
the people of God would be protected and secure within these
walls. Several locations mentioned in the list of repairs hold
spiritual significance far beyond what the rebuilders could see at
the time of their effort.

For example, Nehemiah 3:15 speaks of the repair of the wall
at the Sheep Gate (also: Pool of Shelah (ESV) or Siloam (NIV)).
In chapter 5 of John's Gospel, we find Jesus visiting Jerusalem
during a Jewish festival. In John 5:2-3, the pool by the Sheep
Gate is mentioned along with individuals who are blind, lame,
and paralyzed lying nearby. Jesus sees one man in particular,
who the text says had been there for 38 years. The man was

paralyzed and had been waiting nearly four decades for someone to help him into the pool, which was believed to have healing powers when the water was stirred. No one had ever been willing. Someone always got to the pool before the man could drag himself there.

> *"Get up," Jesus told him, "pick up your mat and walk."*
> *Instantly the man was healed and began to walk (John*
> *5:8-9, CSB).*

This wasn't Jesus' first miracle of healing, and it wouldn't be His last. Yet, its location was a call back to Nehemiah's crew, for, without them, the wall and its gate might not have been rebuilt.

REBUILDING THROUGH COMMUNITY

Do you want to get well? This is the question Jesus asked the paralyzed man at the pool near the Sheep Gate.

Do you want to get well? I asked myself. I decided that I did.

I began seeing a counselor in mid-2017. I had avoided it before then because I knew it would be hard. It wasn't that I didn't believe in counseling. It was because it was something I had never done before, and I knew the process would unearth much of the rubble of my story I had not yet sorted through.

When I first began seeing Virginia, my counselor, it was because of the transition I had just made out of school psychology and into... well, I still didn't know what. Even one year later, I was still rebuilding my identity and needed help figuring out who I was.

After a year of counseling, a new problem emerged as my health spiraled out of control. Most days, I felt like I was walking against a strong headwind or through a tub of peanut butter. I tried to move forward, but the resistance was too great. In the process, I felt like everything I knew to be true was blowing away or getting stuck deep in the vat. When I looked at myself, I saw failure, not accomplishment. My "didn't do" list always seemed longer than my "done." I was stuck, and I needed help.

I am grateful Virginia was there. Someone I never knew I needed.

Fight, flight, and freeze. These are the three most common human responses to circumstances or situations threatening our survival, physically or emotionally. They are natural responses built into our brains by our Creator to keep us safe.

My most repeated response to stress and/or crisis is flight. When I feel unsafe, I pull away from God, my community, and even those closest to me, like my husband, kids, and family. I struggle to believe that anyone else could understand what I'm feeling and could help combat the obstacles I face. So, instead of working alongside others, I have often chosen to work independently or to completely avoid tenuous situations or circumstances.

The problem with flight is that it pulls us away from what we most desperately need—connection with God and others.

In addition to trusting that you are worthy of rebuilding, it's important to know that you were not meant to do it alone. Rebuilding is best done in community, with each person doing their part alongside the other.

Don't plan on rebuilding alone; you will need helpers, healers, and allies. You will need to gather a crew to help you as you rebuild.

In my battle with chronic illness, it wasn't until I began telling people about my struggle and reaching out for prayer on the especially hard days that the task of rebuilding didn't seem so daunting. It wasn't until my husband and I sought counseling together in an effort to better understand each other's perspective on living with a chronic illness that I began to feel safe and secure enough to fight the battle that was taking place in my body, mind, heart, and soul.

Months after Ezer Collective, I wrote a list of all my "helpers." Virginia was on the list, of course. But there were others—friends, family, physicians, etc.

I wrote this list before one of my counseling appointments. I had arrived early and rolled down my car windows, feeling the warmth of the sun and the cool temperature on my face. In the months since Ezer, I had stopped asking God for healing, but I still had not intentionally switched to asking for help. *Who could I ask? Where would my help come from?*

I immediately opened the web browser on my phone and searched Psalm 121:1. *My help comes from the Lord. My ezer comes from the Lord.*

The word *ezer* means *helper, one with the power to support and assist.* It is used most often in the Bible in reference to God who protects, supports, and fights for His people. I knew this, yet I had just made the connection that day. I could ask for help, not just from others, but from Him—the only ezer who needed no helper of His own.

God is so kind. He knows just what we need.

My life wasn't perfect, but as each season of rebuilding ended and another began, God continued to give me words and/or signs that let me know that He noticed, had a plan, and had not missed a detail.

I was at Hume Lake again. It was the fall of 2017.

For several months I had been studying the book of Joshua. One of the themes from that book is centered around the word *remember*.

The Israelites were a forgetful people. Even though God had granted them victory over their enemies multiple times and continued to be faithful to the promises He had made them, they continued to forget Him. It's not that they didn't remember that

He existed, but rather they failed to recognize the order that He had established, which caused their loyalty to become divided. They did what was right in their own eyes, ignoring the boundaries God had set for them and taking and misusing people, places, and plunder that God had set aside for destruction.

As I prepared for the retreat that year, once again as the leader of the group of women from my church, I believed that the theme of remembrance was what I was meant to share. I wrote each woman a letter and gave them a small, smooth stone as a symbol of remembrance, just as Joshua had done for the people of Israel to help them remember.

Each night of the retreat, as I entered the chapel, I found myself looking for signs that God would do what He had done before at previous retreats. Each time I entered the chapel with my heart full of hope, I believed God would overwhelm me with His kindness as He had often done. I had prayed for it specifically and was expectant, confident that He would show up big.

I was in a place of darkness and needed to be overwhelmed by Him. My physical symptoms of pain and fatigue were increasing, and with that came a decrease in my mood. I felt myself falling into depression again. Even though I had begun seeing a counselor, the grief of my transition away from education was still present, and I still had nothing new to show for my time in this new space.

On the final morning of the retreat, I was disappointed with myself for being so sure of what would happen and at God for not showing up as I thought He would. When I walked into the chapel for our last time together as a large group, I was in awe of what I saw. The entire front of the stage was lined with rocks. Wow, God!

It is so hard for me to put these experiences into words, to explain how it feels when this happens to me. When God sees the need of my heart and my time with Him and uses them for His glory. I can't explain why He does it, but I know He does.

At the end of our final session, the speaker instructed us to get a rock and write a word that God had been speaking to us that weekend. I wrote these words: "I am with you."

I needed those words from God on that October morning in 2017, but I would need them, even more, the following year when my physical and mental health worsened. God had not only been meeting my immediate needs at the retreat that weekend, but He had also been preparing me for what was to come. As much as I needed to hear His voice speaking to my present, I needed those words for my future even more.

Remember

DEFINITION

To bring to mind or think of again; to keep in mind for attention or consideration.

A DEEPER LOOK

Look back to look ahead. To remember builds momentum for the future.

VERSE

"We can rejoice, too, when we run into problems and trials, for we know that they help us develop endurance. And endurance develops strength of character, and character strengthens our confident hope of salvation. And this hope will not lead to disappointment. For we know how dearly God loves us because He has given us the Holy Spirit to fill our hearts with His love" (Romans 5:3-5, NLT).

SIX
Work + Fight Go Together

THE WAITING area looked like something right out of the
1980s. Dark brown paneling, light wood furniture, brass lamps,
forest green floral couches, and burgundy wing-back chairs.

I had been there many times before. My journey in counseling began in the summer of 2017, the summer after my big
transition from one career into...well, I didn't know what. I had
likely needed counseling before but had never taken the step. It
seemed too daunting to find the "right" counselor. How does
one even go about that?

It was the following summer, and I was still in the same
place. My counselor, Virginia, was a gem. Older than me in years
and wisdom, kind and gentle, encouraging, and the best listener.
It just goes to show that you can't judge a counselor by the
decor of the waiting room.

Sitting on the oversized 80s-era sofa, I felt physically drained
and mentally discouraged. My mind was racing with all that had
been happening over the past few months—the physical pain
and fatigue and the toll it took on my mental and emotional
state. To make matters worse, it had begun to spill over into my
relationships. I didn't want to be the mom who couldn't have a

game night with her kids—the one who spent most of her time in bed instead of interacting with her family.

It was in that place that I got a prompt from God. He wanted me to write a list. I had already written a list of all the physical, emotional, and mental health problems I had been having over the past few years and when and how they had worsened. I wanted to have it somewhere that I could find easily.

God's prompt, as usual, was something I didn't expect. *Make a new list.* This list would not be about all the brokenness or challenges but all I had seen God do in the same timeframe. *"I'm sure there will be nothing on it,"* I replied.

"Do it anyway."

I made the list. Right there in the waiting room. I pulled out my phone, and below my "problem" list, I wrote all the ways I had seen God move in my life since 2014. All the ways He had partnered with me over those four years. The list was surprisingly long. When I put the second list up next to the first one, I was overwhelmed and wondered how I could have missed this. The ways God had worked in and through me, even while I was at my lowest, were remarkable.

God didn't just want me to remember the hard stuff. He also wanted me to recount and remember the ways He had worked in my life. The ways He had shown up in my weakness and made His name known.

I had a new sense of purpose that day. Looking at the list of problems had made me want to give up. But that second list gave me a new reason to fight.

Most of my growing-up years happened in the 1980s. Have you seen those memes on the internet that say, "You're a child of the '80s if..."? And below it is something pictured or written that is classically '80s. I'll spare you (and myself some embarrassment) by not including a photo of my Orphan Annie afro and braces with headgear. But a few of my phrases would be:

- Telephoned the local toy store daily to see if they had Cabbage Patch Kids in stock.
- Saw the movie Ferris Bueller's Day Off in the movie theater.
- Wore a button that sported Michael Jackson's face and the word "Beat it" on my jean jacket. (I had one with a headshot of Lionel Ritchie and one with My Little Pony, if that gives you a mental picture).

One of the things I was good at as a child was memorizing song lyrics. It was probably because my sisters and I played our records incessantly, singing and dancing around our bedroom and performing our best sets on the hearth of my grandparents' fireplace. These memories of my youth—and the song lyrics—have never left me, so when I began to write this book about the need to fight, Michael Jackson's words came to mind: "I'm a lover, not a fighter."[1]

I'm almost certain that the phrase did not originate with Michael Jackson, but since my husband and I were both huge fans in our younger years, I couldn't resist quoting the king of pop instead of the various others who, according to Google, have also used that phrase.

No matter who said it first, something is inspiring about that phrase. Don't you want to be someone known for loving more than fighting? I know I do.

In rebuilding, though, there will come a time to fight and stand against the adversaries in your life—both external and internal. I've discovered through rebuilding that utilizing the fight within us is even more important in seasons that feel especially dark, when we feel helpless and our power seems limited because it's in these times that fighting gives us hope.

It is in seasons of tension, crisis, and despair that we are forced to ask, "Can God be trusted, even in *this*?" and we must choose our response not based on our circumstances but on His faithfulness in the past and His promises, which secure our hope and inheritance for the future.

I STOOD ALONE and looked at the sea of faces around me. *Do I belong here?*

Imposter syndrome had been hitting me hard since the plane took off from my smallish California town en route to Orlando, FL. I was headed to an event with other women leaders. I had paid for the event, plane tickets, and hotel room, yet still didn't believe I was a leader...at least in the same way these other women were.

My mind had been filled with disorder and chaos before the trip. I felt like I was losing all rational thought and could not understand how or why. I would find out much later (like six years later!) that it was one of the early symptoms of fibromyalgia. Yet, September 2015 was the first time I had experienced anything like it. My word-finding skills were severely limited, and I struggled to make the simplest decisions. My intellectual capacity was diminished, and I felt like I was walking around in a dense fog.

After checking in at the event, I immediately returned to the hotel room instead of hanging out in the lobby and chatting with the other women. I sat alone on the edge of the bed and began to cry. *This isn't how it's supposed to be. What am I doing here?*

Matt had traveled with me to Florida but was not in the room when I returned from registration. So, I sent a text to my friend, Crystal. She was one of the few who knew about all that God had been doing in my life and was someone I could always count on to pray for me in times of immediate need. As soon as the text showed *read* on the screen, my phone started ringing. She was calling me. We spoke for a few minutes, and she prayed for me.

The prayer calmed my nerves and provided clarity for my next steps. I was able to attend the evening session and met a few wonderful women that would remain in my life for years after the event.

That night as I slept, I dreamt. I was on a tour of a large cat rescue facility with my family. On our way to a room where we would hear more about the facility, our tour guide took us through where the lions, tigers, cougars, etc., were kept in cages. There was no fear or reluctance in me. It was as if I didn't consider these animals a threat. Not just because they were in cages, there was another reason, but I couldn't put my finger on it. It seemed strange to me watching this all take place, but not to the me in the dream.

The dream continued, and our group arrived in a small room that appeared to be an office. Several chairs were situated in a circle, and we all sat down. As the tour guide shared information about the cats and the facility, one of the large cats walked into the room. It was obvious by the look on everyone else's faces that they were alarmed. Yet no one said anything. But I wasn't bothered at all. It was almost as if I didn't even notice the animal walking slowly throughout the room, weaving itself in and out of the circle of chairs.

Even as the animal got closer to me, I didn't react; everyone else appeared to have calmed down as well. Then, without warning, the animal jumped at me and latched its jaw onto my throat.

I woke up instantly, short of breath and with my heart pounding. *What was that?!* I knew immediately that this was a message for me. Later that morning, I was directed to 1 Peter 5:8:

> *Be sober-minded, be alert. Your adversary the devil is*
> *prowling around like a roaring lion, looking for*
> *anyone he can devour.*

Who is the lion most likely to devour? The one who isn't ready for it. The animal will target the one who has ignored the threat and has made it easy for the lion to get close and invade his/her space. Jesus spoke to this idea in Luke 11:14-28. After driving out a demon, Jesus was criticized by the crowd and called "the prince of demons" (Luke 11:1). Jesus answered their false claims with several different examples, one of which is found in verses 23-26. Jesus shares a story of an impure spirit that has been cast out of someone and is seeking a place to rest. At first, the spirit only finds places that are void of potential. Without a suitable resting place, the impure spirit returns to the "house" from which it had been cast out. Luke 11:25-26 reads,

> *When it arrives, it finds the house swept and clean and put*
> *in order. Then it goes and takes seven other spirits*
> *more wicked than itself, and they go in and live there.*
> *And the final condition is worse than the first.*

This was the truth of my story. Over time I had become too complacent with the enemy. Not only that, but I had made a comfortable place for the enemy (and his friends) to land, a welcoming environment that they could enter without any hurdles to jump over or walls to tear down. I had stopped fighting defeat and allowed lies to overwhelm my thoughts and cloud my vision. The message became clear: It was time for me to wake up. It was time for me to fight!

FINDING HOME IN JERUSALEM

As the leader of the rebuilders, Nehemiah saw the need to fight. He saw the need to battle the enemy attempting to tear them down, mocking and ridiculing them and threatening violence against them.

Each time opposition came against Nehemiah and the

people of Israel, they sought God and executed a battle plan. They persevered in the important work of rebuilding and were prepared to fight. They were persistent and practical. They continued the work God had called them to do, holding their tools in one hand and a weapon in the other. They trusted God and were prepared for attack. They were a community of rebuilders *and* fighters whose foundation was God alone.

In Nehemiah 4:14 (AMP), Nehemiah encourages the people to fight alongside God and for their future as they continue to rebuild. He wrote,

> *When I saw their fear, I stood and said to the nobles and*
> *officials and the rest of the people: "Do not be afraid of*
> *them; [confidently] remember the Lord who is great*
> *and awesome, and [with courage from Him] fight for*
> *your brothers, your sons, your daughters, your wives,*
> *and for your homes."*

REBUILDING THROUGH WORK + FIGHT

Perceive. Receive. Respond. God revealed these three words to me as He drew me back to Isaiah 43. I was there in 2016 when God was moving me through the wilderness of relearning my identity. *Who was I without an official job or title?*

This time, though, what God was teaching me was different. He asked me to perceive, receive, and respond to His love and choose Him as the source of my identity. This time as someone with chronic pain.

The book of Isaiah chronicles the Word of the Lord through the prophet by the same name. It's in Isaiah 43 that God calls His people back to Himself.

Earlier in the book, in Isaiah 9:7, the prophet proclaims that God did not just create the world and its inhabitants and then leave it. He stayed present to sustain all that He had created. To supply, nourish, strengthen, and support.

God had promised His people rebuilding and, ultimately, restoration. But He never said it was going to be easy. It would require work and fight. And, more importantly, it would require a reliance on Him. In Isaiah 43:2-3 (CSB), we get assurance of challenges when the prophet writes,

> When *you pass through the waters, and* when *you pass through the rivers, they will not overwhelm you. You will not be scorched* when *you walk through the fire, and the flame will not burn you (emphasis mine).*

Furthermore, the Apostle Peter said,

> *If you find life difficult because you're doing what God said... trust Him. He knows what He's doing (1 Peter 4:19, MSG).*

You will continue to need God and others because rebuilding your life will likely bring opposition, just as it did with the nation of Israel. They needed to rebuild the city walls to defend themselves against anyone who might want to interfere with and interrupt their way of life. If you want to be ready to fight opposition and not be deterred, anticipate challenges, and expect provision from God along the way.

But remember, the power of God is stronger than our enemies, even though we can't perceive it.

In 2 Kings 6, the king of Aram was angry at the prophet Elisha, for he had warned the king of Israel of the Aramean army's upcoming attacks. The king and his army surrounded where the prophet Elisha was staying. His servant was afraid when he saw the enemies had come to capture Elisha. Elisha told his servant, "Don't be afraid, for those who are with us outnumber those who are with them" (v. 16).

Then, according to the prayer of Elisha, the Lord, in His almighty and miraculous power, opened the eyes of the servant. He could see that "the mountain was covered with horses and chariots of fire all around Elisha" (v. 17).

Hundreds of years later, the one called Jesus would open the eyes of the blind. And, through His death and resurrection, Jesus would achieve victory over the enemy of the soul. This is the enemy Jesus called the "father of lies" (John 8:44) and the one who He said had "come to steal, kill and destroy" (John 10:10).

Even amid the lies and dark places where burdens are heavy, where you feel inadequate and unknown, and where despair seems like the only way, God says,

> Do not fear, for I have redeemed you; you are
> mine. I have called you my child *(Isaiah 43:1)*.

Do you perceive it?
Do you receive it?
How will you respond?

AT THE END of my son's kindergarten year, I breathed a sigh of relief. We had made it!

However, my relief didn't last long because it was time to prepare for first grade. We knew who his teacher would be, so that was a big plus. But a few things would be different in first grade than in kindergarten. Among them were a larger playground, a longer school day, and eating lunch at school in the cafeteria.

What you need to know about my then six-year-old boy was

that because of his hypersensitive sensory system, his reaction to smells was out of the ordinary for those his age. We had to be careful what we cooked at home, the places we visited, and be prepared for Thursdays at school when the lawn maintenance crew came to cut the grass.

I had worked in schools for many years and knew that the smell of the school cafeteria was rarely pleasant. The combination of pre-packaged, ready-to-eat-and-serve food, along with hundreds of little bodies, could have been better. Even the average nose could sense something was off. But my boy, well... I was worried that the smell would prevent him from eating and overwhelm his system, activating his gag reflex.

Unlike the other changes he would experience, there was nothing I could do to prepare him for the cafeteria experience. I was out of ideas and knew only one thing left to do. Pray. Hard.

My prayer was,

God, take away my son's sensitivity to smell while he is in the cafeteria so that he can eat his lunch and not be distracted.

Toward the end of the first week of school, I asked him how the cafeteria smelled. He seemed confused as he said, "It doesn't smell like anything. It's fine." A school cafeteria that has no smell? My prayers had been answered with a miracle.

When I became aware that there was no longer anything I could do, I realized that I needed to receive what God wanted to give me, even though I didn't know what it would be. I knew a solution was not possible without His intervention. There was no other way. My only choice was to lean into Him and respond to who I knew Him to be.

When we can no longer do anything, our only response is to cry out to God and expect Him to answer. But why do we wait so long? Why do we needlessly bear the pain, concern, and brokenness He has said He would bear? Why do we walk in circles, chaos, and confusion when God can bring order with His word?

FINDING HOME IN JERUSALEM

Nehemiah 4:20 (CSB) says,

> *When you hear the blast of the trumpet, rush to wherever*
> *it is sounding. Then our God will fight for us.*

When we are scattered, we are weaker, making it easier for the enemy to attack. We are so much stronger when we are united—with each other and God.

The enemies of Israel were no match for God. The success of Israel came from their confidence in God, not in themselves. He had faithfully fulfilled His promises many times before, and He would do it again.

For Nehemiah and the nation of Israel to take hold of the promise, to move toward the home that God was calling them to, meant both working and fighting. Nehemiah shows us that the work and the fight go together. The work and the fight belong to the community, not just the individual. We don't rebuild alone.

Believe

DEFINITION

To consider to be honest or true; to accept the word or evidence of.

A DEEPER LOOK

To believe is to move toward God, even in uncertainty. It is a habit, a practice. To allow faith to be our way of knowing. Belief involves action. It is marked by things unseen.

VERSE

Those who trust in the Lord are like Mount Zion. It cannot be shaken; it remains forever. The mountains surround Jerusalem and the Lord surrounds His people, both now and forever" (Psalm 125:1-2, CSB).

SEVEN

Rebuilding Reveals Vulnerability + Hope

I BEGAN to study the theme of rebuilding in the fall of 2019. I was working on a project for a group of individuals I was serving at a local non-profit organization that was (and still is) near and dear to my heart.

I desired to create a biblical-based curriculum that provided tools for individuals who had experienced trauma—specifically in the realm of human trafficking—to rebuild their lives.

One of the primary characteristics of those who find themselves victims of human trafficking is vulnerability. It is this vulnerability that the trafficker uses to woo or lure the individual away from their family and friends and leads the individual to submit to a life of forced labor.

For survivors, moving toward physical, emotional, mental, and relational healing requires building a new sense of self, connecting with others, and establishing new skills. There is also a need to seek help and hope when it feels like there is "no way out" and to break away from old, familiar, and comfortable patterns and rebuild something new.

I saw her immediately when she walked in. I was seated at the registration table, so I knew she would have to pass by me before entering the sanctuary where the event was held. I diligently avoided her "friend request" on Facebook over several weeks. I knew the space she was in when our connection had been severed; she was rebuilding her life and eager to tell everyone about her faith. But that was nearly a year ago. I couldn't avoid her but feared where this interaction would go.

Our time together that day was brief. We only had that one encounter when she gave me her business card, which I politely put into my bag as I thanked her. It was eight months later before I thought of her again.

The prompt came from the speaker at a women's retreat at Hume Lake. She asked us to choose "one thing" to do when we got home. One thing that would help move us toward the next season of life God had planned for us. I knew instantly what my "one thing" would be. It would be calling her.

Her name was Debra, and she was a parent I had worked with as a school psychologist. What I knew about her then wasn't good. She was an absent mother and addict who only showed up at the school when she had a gripe or wanted to make a point. I knew from her business card that part of her rebuilding was starting something new, a non-profit that served individuals whose lives had been impacted by human trafficking.

It was to that organization and Debra that God was calling me as part of my rebuilding journey.

The week I returned from Hume, I accepted Debra's friend request on Facebook and sent her this message:

> I am so grateful that we have been able to reconnect via social media. I am enjoying seeing how much your kids have grown and what nice young people they seem to be. I am also intrigued by your ministry. God has been speaking to me about becoming involved in ministry related to human trafficking for some time now. I have explored a few different avenues, but none have seemed to be the right fit.

I would love to get together with you and see how I may be able to minister to you or the women you are working with. I am no longer working in the school system and am looking at other ways to use my gifts. My biggest passion right now is connecting women with God and each other.

Hoping we can get together in the next few weeks, maybe toward the end of October. Let me know if you would be interested.

We set up a phone call, in which Debra's first words to me were, "I knew you'd be calling." Just three months later, I began to teach classes at her organization.

FINDING HOME IN JERUSALEM

Sometimes we have to fight against external opposition—seen or unseen. People, places, and situations outside of us that are unsafe. Those trying to knock us down and pull us away from the promises of God. Our body is built to recognize and respond to these threats.

Sometimes, however, the opposition comes from within ourselves.

After fighting resistance from their enemies outside the camp, the nation of Israel began to fight within themselves. The narrative doesn't speak of their internal battles but of the tension between individuals within the community.

Nehemiah 5:1 says there was a "widespread outcry" because some of the more esteemed and well-to-do Jews were taking advantage of the poor, using their power to put them in bondage. It wasn't the rebuilding of the wall which created this vulnerability. However, in the process of rebuilding, the heart and desires of the people were revealed. Unfortunately, their heart was not representative of God's heart. The ones created in God's image no longer bore the imprint of His desire for justice.

Throughout His law, God used real-world examples from the culture of the ancient Near East to explain principles of justice, preserve the dignity of the poor and oppressed, and shape the Israelite's view of and heart for humanity. God reminded His people frequently throughout the law that they had been under bondage in slavery, oppressed by a people group who had dehumanized them and made them labor under harsh conditions. And that it was God who restored their dignity by bringing them out of slavery. The Israelites should do likewise; they were to be agents of change and bring His order and justice to a world full of disorder and injustice.

Israel had gone against God's law before, and they were doing it again. This time, as they moved away from God, sin moved through their camp as an infection and slowly became normal—they began to enslave each other. This went against God's plan for their restoration (Exodus 21).

Nehemiah was once again compelled by compassion for this broken people. With a desire to do what was right and just, Nehemiah gathered the community together and addressed the injustices that had occurred. In addition, Nehemiah attempted to do what the people themselves hadn't, to secure the welfare of the most vulnerable among them.

Nehemiah reprimanded the people and demanded that they "walk in the fear of God" (Nehemiah 5:9), releasing their misaligned beliefs about the poor and vulnerable among them and aligning their hearts with God's. In addition, the accused were required to return all they had taken from their fellow Jews.

REBUILDING THROUGH VULNERABILITY + WITH HOPE

The human body is fragile. We are vulnerable and easily wounded.

That's the way we were designed. Because without fragility

or weakness, we would not need God's power. And without fear or uncertainty, we would not need faith.

Fragile is defined as *easily broken or damaged; delicate or vulnerable.*

For me, fragility meant something different. It was more than just my temporary body that I was struggling with. It was how I felt in mind, body, and spirit. Like just one more thing, one more decision would take me from surviving to succumbing. I was afraid I couldn't maintain the pace and the pressure I had put upon myself. Worse yet, some days I was afraid because I didn't even want to try.

I was fragile, and I needed help. I needed to begin to feel strong again. To move toward thriving instead of merely surviving. To allow the light to seep through the cracks in my dysfunctional earthly body. I didn't know how this was possible and needed my faith to be my way of knowing. To believe in what I couldn't see—God's presence. To trust that when I was "feeble and overwhelmed by life," I could find safety and shelter in God alone (Psalm 61:2, TPT).

Being fragile is part of the human condition. Our bodies are not meant to last forever. They are temporary and will one day be replaced with "an eternal body made for us by God himself" (2 Corinthians 5:1). In 2 Corinthians 4, Paul writes that we are like fragile clay jars containing a great treasure (v.7). This didn't make sense to me. I didn't want to be fragile or frail. *Why was this how God had designed me?*

> *So that the grandeur and surpassing greatness of the*
> *power will be [shown to be] from God [His sufficiency]*
> *and not from ourselves (2 Corinthians 4:7, AMP).*

If this is true for us as humans, this must have been true for the human part of Jesus. The part of Him who knew pain and weakness, suffering, and the processes of obedience and surrender because He experienced these to the fullest extent. The crazy thing about Jesus' experience of pain is that it is because of His pain and suffering and by His wounds that we are and will be healed of ours (Isaiah 53:5).

Prior to His death, Jesus encouraged His disciples with what they would need in His absence. In John 14:27 (MSG), He said,

I don't leave you the way you're used to being left—feeling abandoned, bereft.

They were left with healing and peace. It's not a fragile peace that can be disrupted or broken. It is God's peace, which is complete, perfect, and unshakeable. They were also left with a gift, the Holy Spirit, who would make His home in them. These are our promises too.

When we make our home in God, His versions of justice, compassion, and mercy become part of our normal.

There are always things you cannot see. Things that will surprise us about ourselves and others. The more I take time to listen to the stories of others, the more I know this to be true. Unfortunately, much of the learning in our culture and communities has taught us that our posture toward others should be influenced and often determined by the question, "What's wrong with you?"

Instead, what if we change our posture to reflect these questions: "How can I help you?" or "What do you need?"

When vulnerabilities are revealed in rebuilding, we have two choices. We can either make judgments and "should" ourselves or we can adopt the posture of God toward the vulnerable, poor, and oppressed by offering ourselves a bit of compassion. As a Franciscan priest, Richard Rohr so beautifully wrote,

Everything belongs and everything can be received. We don't have to deny, dismiss, defy, or ignore. What is, is okay. What is, is the great teacher.[2]

The question becomes, are we ready to receive what God is trying to teach us?

FINDING HOME IN JERUSALEM

The work was almost complete. The gaps in the wall had been closed, and the city gates and doors were ready to be installed. Nehemiah and the people were almost there, so close to completing their part of God's mission to rebuild the walls of His city. But the enemies—Sanballat, Tobias, and Geshem the Arab—continued plotting against the success and prosperity of their Jewish neighbors.

They used intimidation to put fear into the people's hearts. They schemed to harm and discredit Nehemiah and spoke against the weakness of all people—a tendency to avoid challenging tasks. The people's fatigue and fragile nature could have led them toward despair. Instead, Nehemiah spoke directly against the enemy's tactic:

> You want our hands to be so weak that we stop
> working, stop fighting. I'll show you. Lord,
> strengthen our hands. Make us firm in our
> resolve to work and to fight.

And then, in the next breath, Nehemiah asked God to remember their enemies, to have mercy on them because of their brokenness.

REBUILDING THROUGH VULNERABILITY + WITH HOPE

Sometimes it feels hard to be in the light, vulnerable and exposed. The dark often feels soothing and comfortable. But we weren't created for darkness. We were created for light.

I have this thing for lighthouses. I've been fascinated by them for as long as I can remember.

There is just something about them that draws me in. I guess that's the point, though. They are designed to be beacons. To guide. To help you find your way to safety, your way home.

During my travels in the summer of 2019, I found two lighthouses.

The first was at the end of a physically and emotionally difficult week. I had spent several days in bed, in a dark hotel room in the middle of Times Square in New York. As I lay alone and listened to worship music, the word that I heard over and over was *hope*.

After this word repeatedly appeared in songs, sermons, and social media posts, my curiosity got the best of me. Still in the dark, with the curtains pulled tight, I used the light from my computer to do a word study. I discovered that the word *hope* (*tiqvah*) was also used in specific texts to mean *cord or rope* (Bible Hub).

This correlation took my word study journey to Jericho and an unlikely woman named Rahab. Rahab's city was full of sin and was about to be destroyed, but she knew of the God of Heaven and Earth and declared her faith in Him (Joshua 2:11). As a result, she was given hope—in the form of a scarlet cord— to hang out her window. That hope would keep her and her family safe from destruction; this is the remnant that would lead to Jesus, our living hope.

I had started the year (2019) with "believe" but found myself holding the end of a frayed rope. My tender, broken faith wasn't enough. I needed more.

As my husband and I wound through the streets of New York City, through tunnels and under bridges, and finally down the path that led to a little red lighthouse, I felt hope rekindled in me. The little red lighthouse was no longer in use but became a marker for me. It was my light in the darkness. I'd had to fight to get there, but I found it. A new word. A new way forward.

Hope is expectancy. It's assurance that help is on the way. It's a cord that cannot be broken, keeping us tethered to the one who will never let go. It's a glimmer of light seen from a distance, even through a dense fog. It's a cord hanging from a window, given to a woman who was only ever taken from.

Sometimes, hope is the miracle we've been waiting for.

FINDING HOME IN JERUSALEM

Despite our brokenness and vulnerability, hope is present. It is with us, just as it was with the Israelites.

God had given them the strength to fight their enemies and to complete the wall, with doors and gates installed and locked. The city was secure, and the surrounding nations had lost their confidence because "they realized that this task had been accomplished by [the people's] God" (Nehemiah 6:16, CSB).

As the narrative continues, there is a shift in focus—from the project of the city wall to the present state of its people. It was time for them to get settled into their new home.

The prophet Zechariah was one of two prophets tasked with encouraging God's people as they rebuilt the wall of their city. His name means "the Lord remembers," and his words reminded the people that God had not forgotten them. He also spoke to them of God's promise to establish a faithful, holy city in which the streets would be full. Though it seemed impossible to the people, it was not impossible for God.

In Nehemiah 7, the people's hope and God's promise became a reality. It was time for the people to be settled into the towns of their inheritance again, the ones that God had given to their ancestors, and they could call home again.

REBUILDING THROUGH VULNERABILITY + WITH HOPE

In the summer of 2018, when I was battling chronic pain to the nth degree, my husband and I were in the middle of a home renovation. For more than six months, the five of us and our dog lived primarily in one room—the master bedroom. During the remodel, the master bedroom became our living room (yes, we did have one of our sofas in there!) and our kitchen, including make-shift shelving and a microwave and toaster, with which we "cooked" the necessities.

This process certainly revealed our vulnerabilities and quirks. We can all laugh about it now. But at the time, we were learning a new definition of a close-knit family.

When we first started the renovation process, there were many items we wanted to keep and little we thought we would change. However, we discovered that building the new looked like keeping only a few things and letting go of the rest. The "new" we hoped for would not happen if we held on to too much from the past and worked to adapt to the changes around it. To get a fresh, new look, we had to keep only the items, structures, etc., that would work with the vision for making a better, bolder space.

Only so much can be accomplished when we are unable or unwilling to let go of old traditions, ways of thinking that are no longer healthy or useful, and the lies that will sabotage God's vision for the new. Although there can be great hurt and pain in letting go, there is also great power. In the release, we have the ability and opportunity to connect with God, ourselves, and others.

We can only truly know ourselves by knowing God. We can only truly love ourselves by first receiving the love of God. By holding on to the hope He brings and embracing His promises, no matter how insignificant or small our progress might seem, and letting go of the rest. Remember, the pace and perspective of God's kingdom are a lot different than the ones of the world in which we live.

The prophet Zechariah encouraged the Israelites not to despise small beginnings (4:10), treat them with contempt, or see them as insignificant. The apostle Paul in 1 Corinthians 1:28 (NLT) said,

> *God chose things despised by the world, things counted as nothing at all, and used them to bring to nothing what the world considers important.*

Only with the strength of God working in and through us can we do hard things. We can do the right things. We can fight with the power to overcome.

As you walk in step with God's Spirit and dive deep into the waters of vulnerability, you are being changed from the inside out. Because of God's Spirit living in you, you have access to a life being transformed from old to new.

Deep begets deep. Love begets love. Faith begets power and freedom.

And, If you don't feel like you can move forward today because you're feeling emotionally or physically fragile, that's okay. Start by leaning back into Him.

Boundary

DEFINITION

Something that indicates or fixes a limit or extent.

A DEEPER LOOK

Boundaries represent your present limit and future inheritance. Present faith and future hope.

VERSE

"Therefore we do not lose heart. Though outwardly we are wasting away, yet inwardly we are being renewed day by day" (2 Corinthians 4:16).

EIGHT
Embrace Limits + Celebrate

IN MY TIME as a student of psychology, I learned a bit about the significance of dreams and their possible meanings. Many theories seemed far-fetched, and I never once used them in practice.

I am someone who rarely remembers my dreams. There have been only a handful of times when I found my dreams to carry more meaning than random thoughts that ran through my mind while I slept.

I've already told you about one of the dreams I believe was significant. The other dream occurred in late 2019, and it helped solidify for me the focus of *boundary* as my word for 2020.

This dream contained only one image, a snapshot of a moment. In the image was a girl about ten years old standing in a large field of flowers. The field's boundaries were not visible; it appeared to go on forever. The girl was small compared to its expanse and had nowhere to hide. She was visible among the flowers. She was vulnerable, yet I knew she wasn't afraid. She was safe and free, despite the expanse around her.

Even though the field appeared to have no end, I knew that it did. The boundary was somewhere; I just couldn't see it.

There was also no well-worn or prescribed path in this field. There was freedom to explore. It felt almost dangerous, without rules. Yet, I believed God was with the girl in the expanse and its exploration if that's what she chose. She was His sheep, and God was her shepherd, keeping her close and giving her an open space to roam, tethered to His protection.

The specific identity of the girl was unknown to me as the dreamer. She was nondescript; her features were almost a blur. I suppose that means she could've been me or anyone else for that matter. She could've been a vision of who God wants us to be. People who do not feel hemmed in by their limits but see them instead as an opportunity to draw from God's abundance.

The truth about boundaries is that they don't have to be narrow and restrictive. They can be wide, deep, and expansive; there can be much room to move. They are not inhibitory but freeing. This is true because they have been given to us by a God who cares for us in the midst of them.

In this wide, wonderful field of beautiful flowers, there was no feeling of shame, no need to hide. There was freedom and safety there, even in its boundaries.

There are seasons, and there is sustaining. There is stress that is positive, even tolerable. And, there is stress that becomes toxic.

The thing about chronic illness is that there is no end or limit to it. It is not only for a season. According to Merriam-Webster, the word *chronic* is defined as *"always present or encountered; continuing or occurring again and again."*

With chronic illness comes grief over all that has been lost or those things never realized.

What I've discovered about grief is that the process is never linear.

Grief is like a long valley, a winding valley where any bend may reveal a totally new landscape.[1]

It involves a cycle of anger and denial, sorrow and bitterness, desperation, and loss of hope.

The physical and emotional pain of grief can take your breath away. Taking time to lament or express the deep pain and sorrow you are feeling regarding the loss and change you are experiencing can breathe new life into the dry bones of your soul. Lament allows you to identify what has been lost and to name the emotions you feel honestly; it doesn't change the feeling, but it helps move you toward accepting your circumstances and greater confidence in God's character. And, if you're not quite ready for that, lament can provide a space for Jesus to come in and weep with you while you wait for God to do something.

The process of rebuilding multiple times in the past ten years has meant I was often lamenting. Over and over again. Most commonly, I grieved the high-capacity woman I used to be. The one who would get up before the sun and did it all—worked, wrote, mothered, taught Bible study, exercised daily, got together with friends... and much more. She was tired, but not like this. She wasn't perfect, but she sure got a lot accomplished.

I was often mourning the woman of yesterday. Instead of extending compassion for the woman of today and moving toward acceptance, I held shame over who she had become. I hated the boundaries she faced. Yet, I was also living in fear of the woman of tomorrow. *Who would she be?*

The truth is that "we lament to stop searching for [answers]."[2] Without searching, we can release the need for explanation or justification. We can allow God to love us the way we are and transform us into the person we are meant to be. That woman of ten years ago, last year, yesterday, a minute ago is me—the woman God created, the story He had written.

In this process of lament, I began to discover what it looked like to grieve my limitations and celebrate the goodness of God in them. Attempting to push ahead without considering what it was doing to my mind, body, and spirit would not serve me anymore. I was beginning to wonder if it ever had. All that striving, earning, and pushing had encouraged me to distance myself from my humanness and hide from feelings of inadequacy.

At the time of creation, we were "infused by God with both potential and limitations."[3] We were made in God's image, but also from dust. Without recognizing our vulnerability, limits, and dependence, we will keep trying to achieve the incommunicable attributes of God—the ones that only belong to Him. The ones we can never achieve no matter how hard we try.

Long before I was sheltering at home in March of 2020, God was speaking to me about what it looked like to set limits and push beyond them.

For God's chosen people in the Old Testament, boundaries defined where they lived—the lines of their land. It was their present home and the inheritance for future generations. It was a limit and also a blessing.

During the first months of the pandemic, I read countless verses in which the words "home," "live," and "stay" were the themes. I don't believe it was a coincidence. As I was forced to stay home, God revealed new ways to see and feel at home in *Him.* Psalm 73:28 is one of my favorites. It says:

> But I'm in the very presence of God—oh, how refreshing it
> is! I've made the Lord God my home (MSG).

There is a tension that exists, however, with the way that God has designed our dependence. It is the pull between finding ways to be intentional and also releasing control while embracing our limits. When we can't figure out how to hold both, we miss out on the true beauty of life with the God who created us in His image and is moving us toward an exchange that will provide us with something even greater than we started with.

The paradox, the tension, is the truth of the gospel. There is light and darkness; one is more fully realized when the other is present. There is joy and grief, confidence and fear, choice and dependence.

In the tension, hope is built, and our faith is strengthened.

Although we are limited, there is no limit to how close we can get to God. We can find our present and future home in Him. We can live and move and find out who we are there.

FINDING HOME IN JERUSALEM

The rebuilding of the wall surrounding Jerusalem was completed in 52 days. In less than two months, the people led by Nehemiah had rebuilt what before had been marked by shame and destruction. They had turned the page on the narrative. As the boundaries of Jerusalem had been redefined, so was the identity of the people as God's, set apart as separate and distinct.

A portion of the Israelite's identity as children of God was found in their family or tribal line. The list of people named in Nehemiah 7 repeats those listed in Ezra 2.

> The repetition of this list confirms God's faithfulness in preserving His chosen people and God's loyal love in bringing them back into the land that He promised to give their ancestors.[4]

This was evidence of God's faithfulness in action.

When all the people were settled in their towns, they came together at the Water Gate for the reading of the law by Ezra, the priest and scribe who had been a part of the rebuilding of the temple and had helped the Jewish people reestablish their connection to the God's word and to worship.

Their time in God's law would bring joy and sorrow, rejoicing and weeping.

REBUILDING WITH LIMITATIONS + CELEBRATION

There was a *before,* and there is an *after.* That's how most of the world (or at least most of the people I know) reference their lives relative to March 2020. The definitions of *before* and *after* are based on each individual's life, location, and circumstances.

Here's what I've learned as time has moved us further away from the *before* and into the *after*: Life doesn't look the same. I am not the same. 2020 changed me. I'm guessing it changed you too.

But as much as our bodies, minds, hearts, and relationships changed due to our suffering during 2020, our identity didn't change. It hasn't changed.

For most of us, March 2020 was the beginning of a season unlike we'd ever seen before—a time of unprecedented relational, financial, emotional, or spiritual struggle. There was a heaviness to endure that year, in which we all experienced the collective trauma of a global pandemic. A year marked by racial injustice, increasing political division, and raging wildfires. So much uncertainty. So many questions. There was loss, change, and grief. And the Church was fractured by all the brokenness. The collective trauma experience included loss, fear, and grief, with anger, hurt, separation, and betrayal thrown into the mix.

I couldn't make sense of any of it. Without many of my normal routines, I had a lot more time to sit and listen to my feelings, to explore their limits and depths. I often found myself reflecting on the *before* with nostalgia and looking forward to better things to come.

In 2020, to keep moving forward, I chose to embrace both despair and hope.

I held the burden of despair closely as it reminded me that I am limited and live in a world full of brokenness. I accepted the hope God offered, as it kept me praying and looking for ways to bring His love to myself and others.

I thought a lot about the kingdom of God that year and what it would look like to break into our lived experience here on Earth. God's vision is for a kingdom that resembles the "it is good" of the garden of Eden, where all those made in His image have everything they need to flourish. In her study on the armor of God, Priscilla Shirer wrote,

> Prayer is the mechanism that brings down the power of Heaven into your experience.[5]

In 2020, I needed the power of Heaven. The world needed it too. We still do.

FINDING HOME IN JERUSALEM

Nehemiah 8 contains a pivotal scene in the spiritual narrative of the Hebrew people. The entire community had settled into their homes; their physical locations had been determined, but their spiritual position was yet to be firmly established.

Ezra, the priest, stood on a high wooden platform in front of the assembly and read from the Book of the Law. According to the book of Deuteronomy, the law was to be read aloud and taught diligently to the people, from generation to generation. However, many generations had passed since that had been done consistently.

As Ezra read to the people, they listened attentively and came to a true understanding of God's Word. Ezra began praising the Lord, and with their hands lifted high, the people in the crowd responded, "Amen, Amen!" and bowed in worship (Nehemiah 8:6).

With their response, the people proclaimed their agreement with all that had been read, embracing their position as servants and of the Lord as their holy King—past, present, and future. As the reading of the Law continued, the people began to weep. They were told several times not to mourn or weep, as the joy of the Lord was their strength (8:10).

In Nehemiah 8:9-12, Nehemiah is one of the leaders who encourage the people to step into the new thing God is calling them to. To set their minds on the joy of the Lord, even while still carrying the pain of the past. He didn't want their grief over what had been left behind to prevent them from seeing God's plan for the future.

Then, they celebrated. It was a celebration described in the Law—a celebration of God's holy dwelling place among His people. It served as a reminder of when the Israelites had been without a home, as slaves and wanderers.

God had brought them home once again, this time from exile. To the strength and joy of His dwelling place (1 Chronicles 16:27). To a new beginning for them as a nation. And, to the place that Jesus would later describe as the location of the beginning of a movement outward to all people, the place from which the "repentance for the forgiveness of sins would be preached in [the Messiah's name] to all nations" (Luke 24:27, CSB).

FINDING HOME THROUGH LIMITATIONS + CELEBRATION

I have always struggled with celebrating. As mentioned earlier, I identify as a one on the Enneagram, The Perfectionist. Or, as I prefer to say, The Reformer. That means I can always find something that needs to be fixed, improved, or made better. I am the team member you both love and hate, the one who finds the small error that no one else can see, and the one who is rarely satisfied because there is always more that can be done.

My need to reform—myself, others, situations, circumstances, etc.—is never-ending. My accomplishment of one goal leads directly to the next one, the next thing that is broken or not quite right. This is how I'm built, and I've come to accept it. But the healthier version of me understands that celebration is important too, even if more needs to be done.

That inner critic, though. It's hard to tune out that voice. It's not primarily the adversary's voice—at least, that's not what I believe. But the enemy does take advantage of that voice, especially when I attempt to dismiss or placate it. The move toward joy, pause, and celebration works best when turning down the volume on my inner critic and sending the enemy away.

I'm not here to tell you to "choose joy" in the traditional sense. I think we've all heard that enough.

What I am saying is that for me, taking the time to celebrate, to smile at myself for a job well done, to tell someone else about a client's progress (without using their name, of course) or my grade on my seminary final, requires that I silence the voice telling me to look for the not-quite-right things and to fix them for just a while. I can zero in on the part that has made all the work of putting my new life together worth it.

Our treasure worthy of celebration isn't comfort or ease. It is with-ness. There is no promise of ease in this life. There are ups and downs, highs and lows. But there is a promise of with-ness. Of God come near. Of Immanuel. That is the gift. That is the treasure. It is our joy in the Lord that is our strength. That through everything, we are never left alone.

Some things, like rebuilding, are ongoing. There's always going to be something to make new.

There is a time for doing, reforming, and fixing. Ultimately, though, it is not my responsibility or yours. It is God's. I have never seen that to be more true than in the years I have struggled with chronic illness, in the years I spent resisting prayer while others prayed for me, on the days when I can't seem to focus, but I end up teaching a class that makes a difference in the lives of others.

It's not because I am a great reformer. It never has been. It's because, over the years, I have learned that boundaries aren't restrictions, and freedom looks more like sacrifice and surrender than it does like making sure that everything—including me—is just right. I can live with empty, open hands because God strengthens and fills them. I can celebrate the wins and use them to bring glory to the One who had the victory long before I was born.

It's not easy. But it is so worth it.

FINDING HOME IN JERUSALEM

After their time of celebration came something much more challenging for Israel. Part of the rebuilding process was also restoring the people's relationship with their God. Although the foundation of their identity was settled, the evidence of their loyalty to their identity was still under construction. As a priest, it was Ezra's mission to help them re-align their hearts with God's and re-establish a system of worship.

One of their first tasks in this re-ordering process was confession. The Jewish people were not merely the instruments of God's rebuilding; they were also a focus of the project.

A group of Levites led the people to confess their sins and the sins of their ancestors, those generations of Israelites who were a part of their history. The sins of their ancestors characterized the Israelites as a people group; they confessed these sins with the hope that they would not be repeated.

In addition to confession, a second group of Levites led the people in another important step of re-ordering and alignment.

They praised God through worship as they recounted His faithfulness in their nation's history.

The fruit of worship is that "the worshipers come to resemble the object of their adoration."[6] The goal of worship, praise, and celebration of what God has done is that we would become more like Him. Our expression of belief, how we show our love to Him—is unique to us; it has been woven into our identity from the beginning.

We are not obligated to do any of this—worship, confession, even rebuild—they are gifts we've been given that aid in our transformation. Not because we're bad or wrong as we are, but because we are dearly loved by God, created in His image, and it's His desire that we would become more like Jesus. That we would be made new.

FINDING HOME THROUGH CONFESSION

A few months into my time serving and teaching survivors of human trafficking, I began to feel convicted. The need for my own confession and repentance became evident.

I believed I needed to apologize to Debra for how I had judged her in our past encounters. While I couldn't remember a specific incident or how I had treated her during our interactions, I knew that my heart had previously held judgment against her as a mother, woman, and community member.

When the time came for us to meet, I began speaking aloud before I could think my way out of this confession. I sat in Debra's office and cried through my apology. I wanted her to know I was sorry that I hadn't seen her then—not really. I had only seen what was on the outside—the vulgar tattoos, absentee parenting, troubled children, etc. I hadn't seen her as she truly was—broken, abused, afraid, and in bondage. I hadn't viewed her from God's perspective, through His eyes.

Debra was gracious and kind and received my apology even

though she hadn't known and didn't believe I had wronged her. Then she said something to me that I will never forget; she said that when she started her organization, she knew she needed "a Sybil." She described all the things she had seen in me in our past, the things I'd always longed for people to see but was never sure if they did. She had seen them.

God had allowed her to see me even when I hadn't seen her.

As challenging as it was for me to sit in front of another person and confess to them my pride and judgment, I knew it was necessary to move forward and build into the new God had for me. I was refreshed as I turned away from my past sin and toward God.

ONE OF THE biggest things that changed for me in 2020 was my relationship with the Church. I was disillusioned and wondered how God could love *this* Church. In this current climate, with its people so filled with strong opinions, tension and its communities divided.

When I asked God what to do, He said, *"Stay."* I believed that meant I was supposed to stay at my local church. Even though it was a place that no longer felt like home, I stayed. And, as of the time I am writing this paragraph, I am still there.

The more I think about the word *stay*, though, especially in light of the search for home, I can't help but wonder if when He said *stay*, God meant this instead: *remain, abide, dwell, stay with me.*

There was a time in my life when I never knew the nearness of God as much as when I watched someone I love pass from this life into the next. In the pain and the sorrow, His nearness felt palpable. In the tension and discomfort, it was His peace, I knew. Now I know that nearness can be felt in other moments as well.

One of my grandmother's favorite hymns was *In the Garden.*[7] We sang it over her in her final days. The chorus goes like this:

> *And He walks with me*
> *And He talks with me*
> *And He tells me I am His own*
> *And the joy we share as we tarry there*
> *None other has ever known.*

The word *tarry* is rarely used in our everyday language in 2023. It means *to linger, abide or stay in place.* Jesus talked a lot about abiding—us in Him and Him in us. His brother Jude did, too, when he wrote, "Keep yourselves in the Father's love as you wait" (Jude 20-21).

God desires us to be settled in Him. To keep our attention directed at Him. In times of celebration and praise. And in seasons of darkness, confession, and discomfort.

Jesus embraced the limits of being human; He came all the way. The light came looking for us. All that He is has become ours.

***

On the top of the page of my journal from March 10, 2020, are three words written in all caps and highlighted: "DON'T HOLD BACK." What I believed was being spoken then was a need for me to shift my thinking around the word "boundary." To extend my boundaries so that they were more in line with the limitlessness of God.

Remember the story from Genesis 22? The one in which God asked Abraham to sacrifice his son, Isaac? In that same chapter, an angel of the Lord celebrates Abraham's willingness to step away from his need to control the future and step toward obedience no matter the cost. The angel says, "For now I know that you fear God since you have not withheld your only son from me" (v.12).

You have not withheld. Don't hold back. These words from the Scripture and my journal page pierced my heart.

This passage held the need for me to push and stretch myself. Not merely to think of boundaries as freedom but as abundance. To operate within God's blueprint for my life instead of my own. To once again surrender the use of my gifts and talents, my voice, and my dreams to the One who had given them to me in the first place. A call to embrace my limits without putting additional limitations on myself.

It was also a call to address the unconfessed and/or recurrent sin that had caused me to hold back. My sins of pride and self-righteousness kept me believing the lie that I knew better, that my way was the right and only way. I had also been holding on to the hurt and anger that came with what I viewed as betrayal; there were people I thought I knew who turned out to be different. The weed of bitterness took root and crowded out the mercy and compassion of God's Spirit within me. *How could I teach others about these things when they were so lacking in me?*

It was confession that healed my wounds and transformed them into scars. It was confession that brought cleansing and refreshing. Laying aside these sins defeated the enemy's lies and gave me the strength to reach for the truth of God's promises.

We can go beyond the boundaries we think we might be meant for because, in God, there is abundance. We have access to it. In Isaiah 54:2 (CSB), the prophet speaks of future glory for the nation of Israel when He says,

> *Enlarge the place of your tent, stretch your tent curtains*
> *wide, do not hold back; lengthen your cords,*
> *strengthen your stakes.*

You are free to dream, to use your imagination regarding

your future. To consult your Creator about the vision He has and where He wants to lead you. To think about the possibilities. To declare what you want. To begin building, even beyond your boundaries. Although the future is not certain, there is a God who is. He wants good for you wherever and whenever you are.

The key to rebuilding is growing firm and secure in what holds you. To be rooted in the love and abundance of God. That is what will enable you to stretch, endure, and enlarge.

Freedom

DEFINITION

The quality or state of being free, such as: the absence of necessity, coercion, or constraint in choice or action; liberation from slavery or restraint or from the power of another; independence; the quality or state of being exempt or released usually from something onerous.

A DEEPER LOOK

Experience and operate in the freedom already given you. This may look like sacrifice and surrender.

VERSE

"One handful of rest and patience is better than two fists full of labor and chasing after the wind" (Ecclesiastes 4:6, AMP).

NINE
Remembering Leads To Surrender

As I entered my year of *freedom,* I began to realize how closely freedom was tied to joy. I longed for both.

Early in the year, God took me back to the book of Joshua. In Chapter 1, Joshua was called to be the leader of the Israelite people after the death of Moses. The Lord promised His presence to Joshua and the nation of Israel. They would be equipped to do all that God had called them to do with His presence among them.

Through His words to Joshua, God was leading me to surrender. To release my tendency to focus on myself and my ability (or lack thereof). God had been asking me to do new things, and the words that continued to come to my mind were: *I don't know how.* Although I had grown to believe that God and I were in partnership, I often forgot that He was the initiator, the stronger party. He had done the inviting. *He* knew how.

Without God at the helm, I was a duck, calm and serene above the water but frantically moving my feet beneath the surface, hoping to get somewhere. I was chasing after the wind, knowing it would be impossible to catch, but I continued running anyway, tired and frustrated.

Freedom and joy would only come when I remembered the power of God's presence in me and renamed what I had called *mine* or *ours* as His.

There is a natural transition as we move from one year to the next.

Moving from 2020 to 2021 was no different. Except that it was. A new year meant a new way of living, right? Our new normal would become new again.

For some, 2020 was a year to forget. To move beyond... and quickly. But as the transition got closer, I was intent on moving away from the urge to charge ahead. I didn't consider 2020 wasted and didn't want to count it all as a loss.

As individuals, we were free to hold on. To take the good of 2020 with us into 2021. To reflect on all that was consistent and consider the people who had stayed and how the pace and schedule helped us.

Some of the good that came from 2020 was found within my very own home. Being *forced* to spend so much time with each other, the five of us—my husband, two daughters, and son—had developed deeper relationships than I believed would have been possible without that time together. At first, we did unique (or strange) things like creating and presenting to each other PowerPoint slides and developing quizzes for each other on Cahoot. We also did more normal things like playing board games and watching movies. A family favorite became *The Sound of Music*. What better 3-hour movie is there to watch when you've got a lot of time on your hands?

These were some of the things I wanted to continue. I longed for how we had re-ordered our priorities to include each other for the foreseeable future.

We were also free to let go. To say goodbye to the unhealthy habits and patterns we adopted. To consider the attitudes and motivations that kept us from being the people we were created to be.

Our lives in 2020 also included these types of habits and patterns. But unlike holding on, letting go of the unhealthy was more challenging. After many months of social connection existing only through a screen, it wasn't easy to transition back to face-to-face interaction. Part of this included letting go of the fears buried deep inside, which suggested that face-to-face wasn't safe.

2020 would end, and 2021 would begin. We didn't have control over that, but we all had the opportunity to choose for ourselves, our families, and our homes what was worthy of taking with us and what we wanted to leave behind.

We could hold on *and* let go while remembering that the moments, days, places, and people that made up our 2020 story were all valuable to our Creator. Although nothing is new under the sun, not a bit of our story would be wasted.

Sometimes we have to let things go so that they can flourish. So that *we* can.

In 2015, I began to settle into the habit of going first. Into the idea that I was a leader.

In February of that year, God birthed in me an idea to gather women leaders from my local area. I was leading in my church and longed to connect and help make connections. I thought other women might want the same thing.

That summer, 15 women leaders from my local area joined me in my backyard for dinner and conversation. It was a beautiful time of connection with women who knew what it was like to lead, who desired more leadership opportunities, and even those intentionally stepping away from a formal leadership role.

Then in the winter of 2015, God gave me these words: *lead loved.* These two words were a message to me for that season. But I believed they were also more than that.

It took nearly two years to fully understand what God was asking me to do with those words. During that time, He continued to show me my own need to lead loved. A need to know and understand His love and to lead from *that* place. He was calling me back to my identity and guiding me toward a place of belonging all at the same time.

In November 2017, I started a ministry for women who lead and called it *Lead Loved*. It had been birthed out of my own desire to connect women leaders with God and each other. My hope each time we gathered was that each woman would gain a greater understanding of God's love for themselves and that they would be encouraged in their leadership and inspired to take action.

One of the most difficult decisions I made regarding Lead Loved occurred in the fall of 2019; I believed it was time for me to give it up. I believed that God had more for *Lead Loved* and that it wouldn't happen if I held onto it and continued as the person leading that charge.

It was hard to let go. But I knew it was the right thing to do for *Lead Loved* and me.

My friend, Dorina, became the visionary of the new Lead Loved team. I remained on the team for two more years. In that time, the ministry saw expansion, geographically and culturally.

In the fall of 2022, the time for release came again. I left the team, leaving Lead Loved in the hands of many capable women who love leadership and are passionate about encouraging and equipping leaders.

Proverbs 16:3 (AMP) says,

> *Commit your works to the Lord [submit and trust them to Him] and your plans will succeed [if you respond to His will and guidance].*

The word *commit* is *galal* in Hebrew; it means *to roll away*. What image does this conjure up for you?

I immediately saw myself sitting on the floor, just a few feet away from one of my toddlers. I held a large rubber ball and gently pushed it toward them as I released it. If they wanted to continue playing, my toddler would do the same. But my kids didn't always understand this; they wanted to keep ahold of the ball. (The word MINE comes to mind). They had to be taught that it was better, more fun, and fulfilling if they let go of the ball and pushed it back toward me, believing that I would know what was best—to either roll it back to them or take care of the ball until it was time to play again.

Was I ready to commit Lead Loved to God, fully and completely? Was I prepared to release my grip on it and roll it away? If the answer was yes, I needed to believe that God would take hold of it, care for it, and give it a fixed and secure place in His story, even if it didn't belong as a part of the story He was writing for my future.

I was only free to let go if I remembered these truths. There was no shame in letting go. There was freedom. And, with God holding it all, it would bring more good and more glory once I did.

Do you remember the game show *Let's Make a Deal*?[1] I think it is still on television today, but the version I remember had host Monty Hall walking through an audience of adults wearing costumes looking for those willing to make a deal with him.

If you haven't seen the show, the premise is this: The game show gives you a prize. Then they ask if you want to trade or exchange your prize for something else. There is a catch, however. What you are trading for is hidden in a box or behind a door or a curtain. You don't know what you're getting in your exchange until after you decide. It could be something of greater value than what you already have. Or, it could be something of lesser value. It could also be something called a ZONK—items that were not only lesser, but foul and unwanted, like piles of trash or cigarette butts.

Watching this show as a kid stressed me out! I never wanted anyone to trade *ever*. I know that's not the point of the game, but I didn't care. In my mind, it was better to play it safe than to risk ending up with an item from the junkyard. I wanted every exchange to be good and fair.

There is an exchange that happens with faith as well. Just like with *Let's Make a Deal*, this exchange requires surrender. It requires a willingness to risk, to allow our weaknesses to be known, and to be open to the possibility of being hurt in the process.

In Matthew 10, Jesus provides His disciples instructions before sending them out on mission. As He nears the end of His instructions, Jesus says, "Whoever finds their life will lose it, and whoever loses their life for my sake will find it" (v. 39). The word used for *life* here is *psyche*, which means *breath, soul, distinct identity*. If you're looking for a right view of yourself, you need a right view of God. This requires surrender, to live His way in His world. It requires an exchange—our life for His, His for ours.

No matter the ups and downs of your story, what you receive in an exchange with Jesus will always be greater than that thing you're holding onto.

FINDING HOME IN JERUSALEM

Although the process of rebuilding the wall of Jerusalem took only 52 days, the process of finding home wasn't over for the people of Israel.

In Nehemiah 9, the community gathered once again. This time, as the Law was read to the assembly, the people began to weep, mourning for their and previous generations' sins.

The restoration of their city and their lives was still in process. The Hebrew word *azab* is used in Nehemiah as the English word *restore*, which means to *let loose or set free, to leave, relinquish*. As God's people worked to restore Jerusalem, they placed it back into His hands. God had given them an opportunity for repentance. By confessing and mourning their own sins and the sins of their nation, God was asking them to put themselves under His leadership.

The Levites led the people in prayer, which recounted the history of Israel and their God's faithfulness, mercy, and compassion. This remembering was a time of relearning for God's people. As they heard their story and relearned God's place in it, they recalled His righteousness (v.33), goodness, faithfulness, and mercy. They rediscovered the truth that creation began with the Creator, the covenant began with the Covenant Maker, and being chosen by the One who made the choice.

As they recounted their history, the people came face to face with the character and work of God. At that moment, their praise was not about how they felt or what they could see. It was based on who God had been for them in the past and who they believed He would be in the future.

Their repentance and relearning brought them to a place of surrender. It also created an "urgency in asking God for forgiveness and requesting a change of circumstances."[2] As the light of God came in contact with the darkness of the sins of the past and present, they came closer to the presence of God among them, closer to their home. Through this process, this remnant that God preserved recovered their breath. They were ready to step into new life and become stewards of the story that God was writing for their future.

FINDING HOME THROUGH SURRENDER

I am a list maker, partly because I get satisfaction from crossing items I have completed off my to-do list. But also because I am forgetful. If I don't write things down, I don't remember them. Maybe that's why God asked me to start a blog in 2012. Because He wanted me to remember, to have a record of the ways He was working in my life during that time. To have a place to document the challenging first years of my son's life so I wouldn't forget what I had experienced. So that I wouldn't forget what He had done. That He had been faithful.

The more I study the Bible, the more I notice the times when God asks His people, His followers, to remember. To look back on what He has done and who He has been for them—to recognize Him as faithful, as One who fulfills His promises—so that they may experience peace in the present and hope for the future.

It was in 2016 that I chose "breathe" for my word of the year. There were several reasons for this choice, but the main one stemmed from the feeling of numbness that I felt within my soul. The lack of passion, the utter indifference to injustices, the waning motivation to act on His behalf. My prayer that year came from Ezekiel 37 and Psalm 57:8,

> Breathe life into me, Lord. Make these dry bones,
> this weary soul come alive. Awake my soul!

As I walked along a familiar path one cold and wet morning in 2016, I longed to feel again, for the ability to breathe deeply and for a renewed wonder. I cried out to God that morning. He asked me to change my prayer... just a little. He wanted me to remember. To look back at the times of desperation and joy in my life and to search for His presence. My prayer changed that morning. It became, *"Remind me, Lord."*

More than simply remembering, God was asking me to bring things to memory and hold them there. Not to let them quickly pass through but to linger. To take time not only to remember an event but also to remember the people and places and the words and feelings that went along with it.

This took work. I didn't want to remember these times. But I needed to to remember Him. To see how He had worked to bind the wounds of my past. To wonder how His heart must have broken when I refused to pray to Him for my son's healing. To connect all the dots, revealing the beautiful friendships He had formed and the connections He had made.

In His last meal with His disciples, Jesus said, "Do this in remembrance of me" (Luke 22:19). Do what? Take the broken pieces of our lives and allow them to lead us to Jesus. To share in His suffering. To look at Christ's broken body and internalize it. And to thank God for the healing it brings.

FINDING HOME IN JERUSALEM

Given what they had learned through their time recounting, confession, and praise, the people of Israel decided to renew their covenant with the Lord. They agreed to live within the boundaries of the covenant they had previously broken, yet to which God had been faithful. They were free to surrender to their God, who was reliable and trustworthy and always true to His promises. Their ability to remember God's faithfulness allowed them to enter into covenant with Him again.

Sometimes rebuilding means starting something new. And, sometimes, it means reflecting on the past and worshipping the God who brought us through so that we can surrender our lives to Him and begin again.

Today's faith is not just for today. It builds momentum for a faithful tomorrow.

Stand

DEFINITION

To support oneself on the feet in an erect position; to take up or maintain a specified position or posture; to endure or undergo successfully.

A DEEPER LOOK

Rooted. Intentional. Trusting God in the place He has put you. The Lord will bring you to your feet. Standing up, Standing out, Standing on, Standing for, Standing in, and Standing with.

VERSE

"Therefore put on the full armor of God, so that when the day of evil comes, you may be able to stand your ground, and after you have done everything, to stand. Stand firm then, with the belt of truth buckled around your waist, with the breastplate of righteousness in place, and with your feet fitted with the readiness that comes from the gospel of peace" (Ephesians 6:13-15).

TEN

New Beginnings + Commitments

I HAD JUST SPOKEN on boundaries for the soul. Yet, my own soul was in knots.

Leaning against the back wall of the auditorium at the retreat center, I felt myself sinking. I sat on the floor, still maintaining the wall as my anchor. My body was too heavy and weak to stand. As I listened to the speaker who followed me, I couldn't help but wonder if I had done enough. At that moment, I doubted everything I had said, how I had said it, and whether its applications reached the heart of the women in the room.

Earlier, I wrote that my intellect is my superpower. Actually, I think that my ability to second-guess is.

When our rebuilding is done in partnership with God, it involves the heart, mind, soul, and strength. It is an undertaking for our whole selves. The person God created us to be, from which everything we do flows. Because of my keen ability to second-guess, I have often questioned God's choice to choose, call, and consider me an instrument for His purposes.

I can only imagine what Mary Magdalene thought of Jesus calling her to be one of His disciples. Not just that, but as the one who would be the first to see Him post-resurrection and then carry the message of His resurrection to the other disciples.

Mary Magdalene's name is mentioned 12 times in the Gospels.[1] She is mentioned as "the one from whom seven demons had come out" (Luke 8:1-2) and as one of the women who traveled with Jesus and His other disciples. Jesus had healed her and helped her build a new story.

Mary's involvement in Jesus' ministry was atypical for Jewish culture then, as women "did not typically carry important roles."[2] Mary was one of the women who was present at Jesus' death and burial (Mark 15:47, Luke 24:55). And, in John's Gospel, he documents an interaction between Mary and Jesus post-resurrection. In the John 20:13-17 account of their encounter, Mary is weeping as she speaks to Jesus, assuming He is the gardener. In verse 16, Jesus says her name with the familiar and gentle sound of His voice, "Mary." At the sound of her name, her eyes were opened.

On the morning of the third day, Mary went to the tomb expecting to care for the body of Jesus. Instead, she was cared for by Him. Jesus gave her a new mindset and mission, "Go to my brothers and tell them..." (John 20:17). Standing face-to-face with Jesus, Mary had once again been changed. Mary went and declared, "I have seen the Lord" (v.18). There was no second-guessing here.

God is not after something from us. He is building our story, His story, in us.

FINDING HOME IN JERUSALEM

As we saw in Nehemiah 9, the Jewish people took advantage of the opportunity God provided them for new beginnings by renewing their covenant with Him.

They made specific commitments to "follow the law of God... and carefully obey all the commands, regulations and decrees of the Lord..." (v.29). They promised to keep themselves separate and distinct from the other nations, specifically about marriage and the keeping of Sabbath, as well as making commitments to support the priests and not to neglect the house of God.

As a group, the nation of Israel loosened their grip on their commitment to God. It wasn't something that happened overnight but through a series of small concessions over generations that frayed the edges of the rope that tethered them to their God and the things He cared about. When they let go completely, God gave them over to their enemies and allowed their exile.

Now that the remnant was back in the place God had set aside for them, and the temple and walls had been rebuilt, they were ready to be tethered to God again. As they took time to remember and consider God's vision for them as a people group, they could recommit to the God who had created and sustained them.

FINDING HOME THROUGH NEW BEGINNINGS + COMMITMENTS

To belong means that we feel comfortable being part of a group. It also means that the group's members generally accept us and believe we are an important part of that group.

When I think of belonging, I think of the disciples. The dozen misfits that Jesus called to follow Him during His earthly ministry. This was an unlikely bunch of students, who by Jesus' simple—but definitely not easy—words, "Follow me," became part of His inner circle, establishing a close, intimate relationship with God in the flesh. They didn't have to change who they were; they had to take one step toward Jesus and allow Him to guide them toward something new.

The fishermen became students and then teachers and writers. The tax collector, who had gone to work for the regime that was oppressing his people, became the one who would proclaim the gospel message to the Jews, the very people he had turned against.

In the fall of 2021, I seriously considered attending seminary. It had been something I'd considered over the years, but the timing, finances, or reasons never felt right. I was also afraid to attend seminary. A portion of my fear was due to that inner critic I told you about. But my other fear was that studying God's Word because I *had* to and for a grade would cause me to fall out of love with it. Rebuilding my experience with the Bible had brought me so much joy over the years and I didn't want that to end.

The more I thought about this particular seminary, the more I believed God was asking me to apply. After I sat in on one of the classes, I knew it was the right place for me. I knew I belonged there.

I recently finished my third semester of study and still feel the same. Although going back to school after almost 30 years has been challenging, and many people don't understand why I would want to be a student again, the experience of being with the community of faculty, staff, and students has been so life-giving. My view of God and His Word has expanded into something new and exciting.

Despite the numerous story arcs and summaries I've had to write and the historical and scholarly jargon I have had to wade through, God has lifted my head, set me on my feet, and given me the desire to pursue learning as a way of experiencing more of Him.

Not long ago, I was walking along one of my favorite paths when I asked God to give me a picture of what it looked like for Jesus to invite His disciples into ministry, into relationship. When I turned my head, I saw something I had never noticed before, even though I had walked this path dozens of times.

It was an old, run-down building—a shack of sorts. I couldn't tell what it had been used for previously. It was currently empty and falling over. The paint was stripped, and the boards that once created a stable structure were warped and torn apart.

When I looked closer, I noticed that it had not fallen over. It was leaning. Being built close to a tree, which was deeply rooted and strong, had kept this building from completely falling down.

When we can no longer stand on our own, we can fall on Jesus. When we are overwhelmed with either awe or the stress of the world, He will be the one to put us on our feet and lift our heads.

We can anticipate His presence, His movement, and His strength within us and around us. And allow His power to be made perfect in our weakness (2 Corinthians 12:9) because He is able to increase within us according to His abundance and our need.

In Jesus, we always belong.

FINDING HOME IN JERUSALEM

God's people were beginning to see that the boundaries God had established had been for their good. They were committing to choose Him.

As the people pledged to adopt God's structure and limits for their lives, the boundaries of God's resting place had expanded, moving beyond the temple to the city of Jerusalem, which was being called "holy" for the first time.

> For the Lord has chosen Jerusalem; He has desired it for
>   His home. "This is my resting place forever," He said.
>   "I will live here, for this is the home I desired" (Psalm
>   132:13-14, NLT).

In chapters 11 and 12 of Nehemiah, a list is given—a list of those who settled in Jerusalem and those who lived within their ancestral towns and villages. The people structured their community and made their home in specific areas of the land according to the design outlined by God when their ancestors had first entered the land that He had promised them. Their names, tribes, and roles in the community were important, not just to determine their assigned inheritance but also to reveal God's perfect and detailed love for them. And for us.

God had chosen an individual and made him into a nation. Yet, each person was still important to God. He knew the name of each one, their family, tribe, and personality. He knew their function within the community, where they had come from, and where they were going. God cared for and cares about the individual.

From the way He knit us together in our mother's womb to His knowledge of our thoughts, words, and movements, God has a thorough and intimate familiarity with us (Psalm 139:2, 4, 13). This is good news!

FINDING HOME THROUGH NEW BEGINNINGS + COMMITMENTS

The women are broken.

I looked around the sanctuary as I heard these words. I saw women of various ages and colors—those with children and without. With the worship music as the soundtrack of my thoughts, I watched and prayed to understand what God was trying to say to me. In addition to the words, I also felt a sense of urgency, as if God was asking me to do something for the women, with them, and soon.

I believed it was about rebuilding. Not much didn't revolve around that theme at this point in my life. On this day, I sensed that these words were about creating space and bringing the broken women to Jesus, showing them the way.

Luke 8:40-56 tells a story of a woman who had been bleeding for twelve years and a young girl of twelve years old. Jesus gives both new beginnings. Although the stories of these two females are intertwined in the Gospel of Luke—which provides us with much more to unpack than we have the space for here—I want to focus on the woman, as I have found hope for my own story in hers.

When Jesus traveled through towns and villages, crowds of people came to see Him. That day, there was a woman among the crowd, one who the biblical text notes had been suffering from some type of bleeding issue for twelve years and who had spent all the money she had on doctors yet was not healed by any of them. Among the Jews, generations of laws and rituals regulated cleanliness and uncleanliness. One of the matters of uncleanness for women, which kept them "out of the camp," was bleeding (Leviticus 15). Because "the great calling of Israel was to be God's holy people among whom He could dwell,"[3] a system had been established by God to provide the Israelites with a way for them, as broken and sinful humans, to remain in the presence of their Holy God.

On His way to the home of a 12-year-old girl, a synagogue leader's daughter who was near death, the woman reached out to touch Jesus' robe from behind (Luke 8:43-44). The woman was instantly healed. Jesus knew that He had been touched, as He had felt the power go out of Him (v. 46). Although the woman had been brave enough to enter a crowd when she was unclean—a big problem in the Hebrew culture—when Jesus stopped to talk with the woman, she came to Him with fear and trembling, falling before Him.

Jesus told her, "Daughter, your faith has saved you. Go in peace" (Luke 8:48).

There is so much significance in these few words alone. Jesus begins by calling this woman "daughter," a term suggesting that she was welcome in His family; she was no longer an outcast; she belonged. As a female who had been bleeding for twelve years, this woman would not have been allowed around people, even her own family, as there was a belief that she could pass along her uncleanliness to them. She had touched Jesus, yet He didn't address the possibility that He had been made unclean by her. Instead, He passed His holiness, His cleanliness, onto her by inviting her into His family. Exactly where she had fallen, He called her to stand.

Jesus also assured the woman that she was freed from her suffering; she was rescued from her physical, emotional, and spiritual brokenness. She had been made whole and would be kept safe and protected because of her faith—her action was evidence that she believed Jesus was the only one who could save her from everything she was experiencing—past, present, and future. He could do for her what no one else had been able to do or would be able to do. With one touch and an invitation, she became free. After this freedom came release, as Jesus sent her off to her new beginning, with new life restored within her.

God's kingdom is meant for those, like this woman, who have recognized their need for Him. Those who, in their desperation and brokenness, are longing for Him to breathe new life into them. The ones who may have heard others give testimony of the things He has done but are yet to experience them. The story of this woman in Luke 8 ends with her healing. We don't know what happened after that. But I have to believe that once she tasted the new life Jesus offered, she wouldn't return to searching for a different kind of cure.

In one of His most famous sermons, commonly known as the Beatitudes, Jesus proclaims a list of kingdom qualities (Matthew 5:3-12). Included in His list are those who mourn, are poor in spirit and meek, and hunger and thirst for righteousness. Also included are the merciful, the peacemakers, and the pure in heart.

We can be none of these without brokenness and need. There is more room for God to move, bless, and favor in our need. There is also more room for true joy—satisfaction, regardless of circumstances.

A new beginning requires longing, the place where God will meet you and lead you to more.

But something else may be required of us as well: sacrifice. We must remove those things that are competing for His attention. It could be doubt, pride, or the need for the approval of others. The voices of political parties, social media, or false teachers. Or unhealthy coping habits, like an over-reliance on food, alcohol, shopping, etc.

In longing, we have the opportunity to change our perspective, increase our faith, and find our hope once again.

We are broken to be healed. Empty to be filled. Our place of pain and longing is the place of sacrifice.

In rebuilding, we must allow God to heal the broken places and fill the hungry places because He is the only one who truly satisfies.

FINDING HOME IN JERUSALEM

When the time came for the wall of Jerusalem to be dedicated, songs of celebration were sung as the leaders of Judah walked the perimeter of the wall. The scene was reminiscent of the conquest of Jericho. In Joshua 6, the people of Israel walked around the walls of Jericho, which fell to the ground, enabling them to enter the land God had promised them for the first time. The wait was over; they would be home after wandering for 40 years.

This time, though, the walls would remain standing. God had brought His people home again, just as He had promised.

His works were awesome and inspired awe and a need to mark the moment with celebration. God had enabled them to rebuild. He filled them with joy and wonder as they celebrated all He had done.

Included in their celebration were purification and sacrifice. In addition to re-establishing their commitment to God's covenant, these rituals were another way for them to recognize their own need and God's holiness and sovereignty over all. They were one step closer to being part of what God had allowed them to rebuild and live there as He had created them to be. They were ready for holy action.

REBUILDING THROUGH NEW BEGINNINGS + COMMITMENT

Two rhythms on the Christian calendar have been meaningful to me over the past ten years: Lent and Advent. Since my first-ever experience with Lent in 2012, I have intentionally included these two rhythms in my spiritual practice each year.

The focus of Advent as a rhythm is one of anticipation and expectancy. It offers a natural rhythm of hope to a time of year that can be chaotic and crazy. The definition of the word *advent* is centered on an upcoming arrival, in this case, the arrival of Jesus.

The truth of Advent is that God is not only calling us away from the chaos and sin of the world, but He is also calling us to Himself. Because He is better. God knows the truth about us… it's challenging to say *no* without having something better to say *yes* to.

Advent 2022 was no different.

In the quiet of the morning on the first day of Advent in November 2022, I felt God inviting me into release and rest. And into a place of wild wonder. I had been longing for slowness, the space to breathe, and the ability to experience God with not just my mind but also my heart and soul. But I had also been longing for something I needed to confess. I had longed for recognition and validation, to know that I was doing things the "right" way. At the moment of confession, I desired to release my rightness and to receive satisfaction in the who, where, and what of my story. And to receive the tension and discomfort of mystery and the unknown.

Before the sun had risen that day, God had invited me to a new beginning: hope. My tasks were simple but not easy: embrace the tension, lean into the longing, make room for Him to work, and make myself available to the holy work of being made whole.[4]

Behold

DEFINITION

To perceive through sight or apprehension; to gaze upon (observe)

A DEEPER LOOK

Look at with purpose; direct our attention without distraction. Observe and consider.

VERSE

"You will be delivered (saved) by returning (turning back) to me and resting (stop striving); your strength will lie in quiet (undisturbed) confidence (trust) (will come by setting down in complete dependence)" (Isaiah 30:15, AMP).

ELEVEN

Rebuilding Is Ongoing + We Are Being Built

IT HAD BEEN SEVEN YEARS, almost to the day, that I'd decided to leave a comfortable place where I was operating in my capacity and knowledge and where my need for God appeared small and insignificant. I wasn't hungry for Him there, and my urge to call out to Him only came when I thought of leaving, when I wondered how it would look if I could no longer answer the question, "What do you do?" with a simple two-word answer.

Here I was again, not in a physical location but in a space where God was calling me to move into the unknown. In February 2016, I was in bed when I heard from Him. In February 2023, I was in a retreat house in Texas, ironically sitting on a bed. But it wasn't about the state I was in or who I was with. It was about the words God was speaking to me—*"I'm taking you to a place where you need Me."*

It was as if God was saying (again): *"You are trying to do this thing on your own. You're too comfortable in your capacity and aren't longing for Me anymore."*

As someone struggling with chronic illness for nearly a decade, I finally settled into a routine and regimen that worked.

I was comfortable with what I could and couldn't do. Too comfortable. I had stopped asking for greater capacity, greater things... because I didn't believe they were possible. I hadn't forgotten about God altogether, but I had eliminated Him from my conversations about capacity, church, and loving Him with my whole self.

As hard as it is for me to say, I wanted to be enough without Him. I didn't want to need Him. I was like a two-year-old trying to put on her shoes but unable to be fully independent at it. I wanted to do it myself and, knowing I couldn't, had given up, frustrated but ready to try again the next day with almost certainly the same result. Instead, I should've been doing it *with* the One who knew how to do it. The One who continued to love me despite my inability to do it on my own. He was ready to help and always available whenever and wherever I chose to call out to Him.

"The great struggle of the Christian life is to take God's name for us, to believe we are beloved, and that is enough."[1] I had been feeling that struggle. To believe and be loved. To behold and be held.

A process that had begun in February 2016 was still at work in me. A process that had moved me closer to God, but not close enough. Because it wasn't just about leaving a career as I had previously thought, it was about keeping me fixed and rooted in something more than my idol of independence.

The seventh anniversary wasn't about completion. It wasn't the end of the story; it was a checkpoint for me. Where was I in the process of rebuilding my identity? Was I abiding in God, finding my home in Him? Or, was I the two-year-old stuck in a place that I had been before and ready to give up?

I had gotten so good at chronic illness; I had mastered it. The days of my life had become habitual. I once again failed to acknowledge the value of being in a place, time, and space where I needed to rely on God. I had forgotten the breadth of

God's love for me. I had never truly accepted and embraced it as He wanted me to.

Why? Because I didn't want to be in that wilderness place where I woke each day and waited for God's manna, just enough to get through that day. I longed to be in the land of promise, feasting and drinking from its abundance. God was giving me enough, but I still wanted more.

I was the seed on the rocky soil.

In Luke 8:4-15, Jesus tells a parable about a farmer who "went out to sow his seed" (v.5). In this parable, Jesus does something unique, something He does with only a few other parables. He gives its explanation. He tells the crowd that the seeds represent the gospel and the soil is the human heart. The seeds are all the same, as the gospel does not change. It is the response of the heart that determines the bounty of the harvest.

On rocky soil, the seed's plant cannot develop roots. This leaves the plant without stability or a connection to its source of nourishment. "A plant in this state cannot endure for long; it withers quickly when exposed to the elements."[2] A heart without roots harvests a faith that cannot be fully transformed, as the word has not fully penetrated the heart, mind, and soul.

> It's not enough to hear the Lord's words; we must carry them. We must always hold and keep His words and allow them to abide in us.[3]

A deeply rooted, nourished faith shapes our desires and prayers. Our answers don't come from our circumstances or feelings but from God's truth.

Here's the thing about seeds. They don't grow unless they're planted in fertile soil. Unless they are nurtured and cultivated. Rebuilding is the same. Both require a level of depth and care.

In Galatians 5:22-25, the Apostle Paul writes to the church in Galatia about the fruit of the Spirit of God. He follows with a passage about reaping and harvesting in Chapter 6. Why? Don't the seeds come before the harvest? Yes and no. Seeds planted in fertile soil are nurtured and cultivated to become plants that yield fruit. The seeds come from the fruit for the next planting season. It's a cycle—a continual sequence of planting, nurturing, fruit, harvesting, and planting again.

Care must be given at the beginning of each new rebuilding season as the soil is loosened, preparing it for its seed. The same is true for us as we sift through the rubble of the previous season(s) with compassion and kindness toward who we were yesterday and who we will be tomorrow. Each day, each step in the process of rebuilding is like water in the soil of bravery, helping the roots grow deeper and providing nourishment for the life you and I were meant to live.

In times of abundance, when the harvest of our lives is plentiful, it is essential to continue the sequence. To plant the seeds that come from the fruit. To give away some of what has been given to us. To continue to pursue our relationship with God and His Word.

> God seems to be stretching us past our abilities, resources, and capacity. It is just past ourselves that we see more of Him and He is best seen through our lives.[4]

If we are too comfortable, we miss our need for God. We never feel the hunger or longing for Him. This is what I had become: comfortable. Comfortable in a career I thought I would spend my life doing. Comfortable in a rhythm of doing what I could do in my own strength... and nothing more.

FINDING HOME IN JERUSALEM

Years after recommitting their lives to the covenant God established with them, the Israelites' resolve changed. While their intentions had been honorable, the soil of their hearts left them with an insecure faith and a weakened loyalty to God's law. This led the Israelites to a place where they violated each of the specific commitments in the covenant they had made with God.

Although they had seen what God had done and participated in fulfilling His promise, they had not allowed wonder to permeate their hearts, minds, and souls. The rituals they had been given to teach them about their God were to represent the way Israel was "meant to act, and therefore, think about the world"[5] and had been abandoned. As a result, the sins of the past resurfaced, and new ones emerged. Their new way of thinking became inaccessible, replacing it with their former ways. Their tendency to follow the idols of the surrounding nations became greater than their vow to follow the Lord as their God. To make their home in Him.

You're tempted to shake your head at the Israelites right now if you're like me. Why aren't they getting it?

FINDING HOME THROUGH PERSEVERANCE

Triggers. They come in all shapes and sizes. They come when you least expect them.

It was the day after my 46th birthday. I woke up in the early morning hours in pain. Pain like I hadn't felt in a while. The day before, I had felt "normal"—able to work all day with plenty of energy—no need for a long break or a nap mid-afternoon.

The 3:00 am pain triggered something in me. At that moment, I was transported to 2018, when I barely slept most nights due to pain.

Triggers are cues or signals from our external environment or within ourselves. They can come from what we see, hear, and smell. Or a pain that originates within our body. They can present themselves through an ordinary activity or something unusual. Sometimes, we can't identify them, but we know they are present by how our heart races, our breath quickens, and our stomach churns. The triggers themselves are harmless, but our bodies don't think so. Because of an imprint left from our past, our mind, brain, and body recognize these harmless cues as threats that require immediate action.

That early morning in March, my body responded to the pain like it had in the past. Immediately, my mind went into panic mode. Suddenly, the familiar—yet long gone—feelings of hopelessness and helplessness came back. I felt sad, scared, and angry. I doubted God at that moment. I questioned Him: *God, what are You doing? I thought we were done. I thought You were with me in this.* I doubted what He was doing and what He could do. I also felt betrayed, like yesterday had been a cruel joke. Like the "normal me" of the day before wasn't me at all.

As I processed all this with God, He whispered to me: *"They are both the real you. It's all you."*

This is what it was like to live with trauma, in my case, from a chronic health condition. When one feeling, smell, touch, or word is identified as a threat, and leaves you feeling unsafe. When survival becomes its main focus, the brain uses all its energy to react, in my case, with flight. I had lost the ability to reason logically and to recall everything I had learned over the years in an instant because of what the pain triggered.

This is what we see happen to the Israelites at the end of Nehemiah. We're left with relapse at the end of their story, at least according to Nehemiah, because even when committed to continuing to build into the new remains, lapses in faithfulness are normal. Apathy, a lack of interest or concern, is a symptom of brokenness. Of an inaccurate or fractured identity. A need to ask for help. Because help is the path to endurance, it is the armor for the battle—the strength to keep fighting.

FINDING HOME IN JERUSALEM

After 12 years of being the governor of Judah, Nehemiah returned to his role as cupbearer for the king of Persia. However, he was called back to Jerusalem and discovered that evil was being done in God's house and God's city.

It hadn't taken long for the Israelites to return to their old patterns.

One year after Nehemiah returned to his post in Susa as the king's cupbearer, the people of Jerusalem failed to keep their commitment to following the terms of God's covenant. Sin had become normal within their leadership and community, and their obedience to God's law had been compromised.

Despite their promise to keep to the Lord's rituals and not neglect His house, they began to do the opposite. And they married their children to those of the surrounding nations. Nehemiah returned to Jerusalem to help the people get back on the right track.

God's Word, in its entirety, is an invitation to us. It has been given to everyone, but only a few will nurture and cultivate it. God may be overall, but just as He did with the Israelites, He's still giving you a choice. He's not going to force you, and He's not going to compete with the other voices or noise in your life.

God desires that you continue to seek after Him as you rebuild into the new. To look forward more than you look back. To show up broken, allowing His power to work perfectly in your weakness. To listen for His voice and respond with humble, authentic obedience.

God has begun a work in you and will not leave it undone!

FINDING HOME THROUGH LOOKING BACK

I was heading into a time of discernment, discovery, and development as part of a cohort of women who were committed to learning about themselves and the way(s) in which God wanted us to carry His Word, the Word, to our people and places. As is typical for me when I enter a learning space, I was eager for new information to emerge.

One of our first reading assignments contained a question that surprised and disappointed me. It was: *"What has God already revealed to you about who you are?"*

This was not what I had expected. I joined this cohort to learn something new, not to rehash old information. Yes, I had been collecting details, facts, and opinions about myself for a long time. I had been learning about who God had created me to be. But I hadn't yet formed an opinion or settled on an answer to the question, "Who am I?"

The more I argued with God about this, the more I believed I was right. Then entered the image of a magnifying glass and the words: *"Take a closer look."*

There I was, smiling and picture-perfect on the outside but overwhelmed and insecure on the inside. I felt lost, wondering what was next, desiring clarity and a spark of something new that would instantly change me—an epiphany of knowledge that would cause the tension that came with pretending to disappear.

> *As you learn more and more how God works, you will*
> *learn how to do your work.*
>
> — COLOSSIANS 1:10, MSG

God wants us to know Him, not to search for the next and newest thing constantly but to take a closer look at who He is. It clarifies who we are and what He created us to do.

Sometimes looking at things with "fresh eyes" means taking the time to remember what you've already seen and felt when the world around you wasn't in chaos or didn't feel like too much.

> *As for you, see that what you have heard from the beginning remains in you. If it does, you also will remain in the Son and in the Father.*
>
> — 1 JOHN 2:24

Consider this... Is it possible that you already know who you are? That the passion or burden necessary for clarity is already inside you? That you already know what God's vision for rebuilding looks like for you? You just have to take a closer look. To reflect on what God has already told you. And then take the next step.

———

I HAD my last counseling session in June 2022. Well, I don't know if it will be my last forever, but for this season.

Most of my last few sessions were 6-8 weeks apart, and I spent most of the sessions catching my counselor up on what had happened in my life since we last spoke. I told her about all I was doing, what I'd stopped doing, and shared about my family, and that's about it. The end of our sessions felt awkward. Things seemed to be going well and I could sense that my counselor wanted to release me. Yet, I couldn't let go. *Am I really ready? What happens if I need her again?* She could sense my questions and continued to extend the time in between until that week.

I wasn't sure what to do after I pushed the end button on our virtual session. I felt like a piece of me—the part stitched inside since the summer of 2016—had just been removed. There was an empty space there. There was grief over what would be lost: the person who mostly listened and never interrupted, who taught me not to judge my thoughts or emotions, who encouraged my interests and never stopped being amazed about all the information I had acquired and the things I continued to accomplish, even when to me it felt like life and progress were moving at a snail's pace.

My counselor was not the first person to do this for me. There was my college professor, who became my interim pastor, and finally, my mentor and friend. He knew what it was to love —"to promote the temporal and eternal best good" of another— and to have faith—"to act as if what you believe is true." He was one of the smartest men I have ever known, yet never tired of dialoguing with others to challenge his faith. He was a constant for me through the years; the one who always stopped to talk, asked the best (and hardest!) questions, listened without interrupting, shared his books and the stage, and never stopped encouraging me to learn, write and grow.

I felt lost when he died. I couldn't imagine who could take his place in my life. There wasn't, and has never been since, anyone like him. I often think of him and how he guided me through many years of my life. He gave as a counselor would give but never asked for anything in return.

In his absence, and now in the absence of my counselor, it is my responsibility to look to the ultimate Counselor for all the things these two people provided for me: the questions, the answers, the encouragement, and the partnership. They took their roles in building me very seriously. Now, it's my turn.

As we rebuild our lives, we are being built.

FINDING HOME IN JERUSALEM

The end of the book of Nehemiah is unsettling. It leaves us longing for more. It leaves us as needy people, looking for a light that is to come.

In one sense, it would have been understandable for Nehemiah to give up on the Hebrew people. However, the final verse of chapter 13 speaks to something different. It is a statement from Nehemiah to God: "Remember me for this also, my God, and show mercy to me according to your great love" (v. 22). I see it as Nehemiah's release. He did what God asked him to do—he led, encouraged, equipped, and prayed for the people. It was time to let them go. Nehemiah came to the end of his mission. He had loved God's people fiercely but had known the necessity of holding them loosely.

Maybe Nehemiah knew something about the truth of transformation; it is slow and takes a lifetime. Nehemiah believed in a God who was a promise-keeper. Although Nehemiah wouldn't see the promise fulfilled, he played a role in rebuilding the city that would be the center of worship for generations to come. Jerusalem is also where Jesus wept and mourned for Jerusalem's inability to see "and recognize and welcome God's personal visit" in Jesus Himself (Luke 19:44, MSG).

Temporary reforms were never the final answer. Nehemiah only held a shadow of Jesus. Rebuilding only holds a shadow of the promises of God. It is our lived reality, but it is not the end of our story. The Apostle Peter said it this way: "And then, after your brief suffering, the God of all loving grace, who has called you to share in His eternal glory in Christ, will personally and powerfully restore you and make you stronger than ever. Yes, He will set you firmly in place and build you up" (1 Peter 5:10, TPT).

Although rebuilding helps develop persistence as we move toward our earthly future and home, it is not our hope or eternal home. That is only found as we live in the love of Jesus and allow His love to live in us (1 John 4:15).

This is our firm foundation, the assurance of life eternal.

FINDING HOME THROUGH GOD'S ABUNDANCE

Some say that God's kingdom is upside down. As part of His kingdom, God is inviting you to a new way of living that is better and harder than the one the world gives. One in which the missing pieces and uncertainty are an opportunity for you to see Him move in ways greater than you can imagine. One in which we are safe and secure but maybe not comfortable.

In Matthew 7, Jesus concludes the Sermon on the Mount with a parable that compares the "wise" and "foolish" builders. This comparison between the wise and the foolish is seen throughout scripture, predominately in the Book of Proverbs, which describes the paths of wisdom and folly through various analogies and other poetic language. Jesus' parable gives us another way to view those who are wise and those who are foolish, but it also helps us understand the path of those who find themselves at home in the refuge of God and those who desire ease and comfort.

> *These words I speak to you are not incidental additions to your life, homeowner improvements to your standard of living. They are foundational words, words to build your life on. If you work these words into your life, you are like a smart carpenter who built his house on solid rock. Rain poured down, the river flooded, a tornado hit—but nothing moved that house. It was fixed to the rock.*
>
> *But if you just use my words in Bible studies and don't work them into your life, you are like a stupid carpenter who built his house on a sandy beach. When a storm rolled in and the waves came up, it collapsed like a house of cards.*
>
> — MATTHEW 7:24-27, MSG

God is offering you the opportunity for safety and security. Freedom during the storms of life, to take your burdens and brokenness to Him, to receive and to learn; He will exchange your burdens for His rest and peace. When you choose to settle into His presence, you will experience His unshakeable goodness, even when the world around you seems to be falling apart.

But God's kingdom is not only about you and me. God is not just asking you to know Him but also to make Him known. As part of God's kingdom, you have been called to bring life to your people and places. To bring change and uniqueness. It is not to withhold the good of wisdom from others; it also belongs to them (Proverbs 3:27).

Like Jesus, you can keep the future in mind even though you have already and may currently be experiencing the effects of sin and/or suffering. You can also show grace and mercy and be moved by compassion for yourself and others. With God as your home, you can become a safe place where the kingdom of God can flourish.

One of my greatest fears is that God is holding out on me. Each day, I fight against a scarcity mentality, one that believes that God's love, gifts, purposes, and provisions are in short supply. That there is something greater "out there" that I'm missing because He has chosen not to give it to me. The same lie that deceived Eve—that allowed her to decide that she wanted to be like God instead of the person He had created her to be—plagues me. Like Eve, I knew how to receive life, yet I wanted something more. I longed for what others had. I found myself constantly looking to the right and left, not for the path God had assigned me, but to discover what those beside me had that I didn't.

Scarcity is not the truth. It's a lie. Don't let the enemy convince you that God is holding out on you. He can do extraordinary things through ordinary people who are yielded to Him and walking in step with His Spirit.

God is good and kind and trustworthy. He gives freely. Just as He wants us to find our home in Him, He intends to make our heart, soul, mind, and strength His home. The best part is that He brings all the materials and supplies we need to transform into a beautifully adorned dwelling place. Our task is to believe this is true and partner with Him in the building process.

Toward the end of 2020, I trained to be a coach. One of the phrases our cohort of coaches heard repeatedly in our training was: "You're not the hero." Although it felt hard to hear at first, it comforted me.

There is such freedom in knowing that I have a greater hope than myself. I don't have to rely solely on what I know or can do. I can be a helper, but I don't have to be the hero. I can do my part, but my part is not the whole. The truth is there is Someone greater who takes my humble, meager offering and multiplies it. A limitless God in whose image I am created and whose nature I can draw from.

If I'm not the hero, if you're not, then there is no limit to what can be accomplished!

If the ongoing nature of rebuilding and its routes are not often direct provides added pressure for you, I want you to know that you're off the hook. You don't have to be the hero of your own story or anyone else's. The pressure is off.

We can get rid of the expectation that it's all up to us. We can do our part intentionally and then lean forward with expectancy, knowing He will move.

TWELVE

Final Words + Words Yet To Come

THE TRUTH IS that the journey to finding home does not follow a straight line. It is a long, winding road from which we get glimpses of what home looks and feels like. Just when we think we've arrived, there is another lesson that needs learning or another loss that needs grieving. But *how* we get there is not as important as the home to which we are headed or who we are moving toward. It's not until we believe that we are carrying our home with us that we can remain secure.

Some animals find their homes in their environments. Others build their homes themselves.

Soft-bodied animals like crabs, snails, and turtles carry a shell as their home; it is part of their body. Much like our physical homes do for us, these shells are designed as a shelter to protect the animals inside from the elements of nature and their predators.

The hermit crab is among those animals that carry their homes. However, it differs from the others in that its home changes throughout its life span, which can be up to 30 years when living in its natural habitat.[1] As a hermit crab grows, it needs to find larger and larger shells to adapt to its new size.

Not unlike the hermit crab, we are meant to grow and change. Life as a follower of Christ is about transformation through God's grace and our faith. As we live each day, each experience, we are being transformed into the image of our Creator and His Son, Jesus Christ, within whom the "fullness of God was pleased to dwell" (Colossians 1:19, ESV).

In the business world, a change agent is defined as "someone who promotes and enables change to happen within any group or organization."[2] In a believer's life, God's grace becomes the agent of change. Although there is a mystery surrounding the full understanding of grace, a simple way to describe it would be as the underserved favor of God, the enjoyment of the benefits He has to offer. This means that all that God has chosen to lavish upon us—His love and mercy and forgiveness, etc.—is a byproduct of His favor. We have done nothing to merit these gifts. We receive them simply because we are His children, called to believe and steward all He has given us with the utmost care and responsibility.

I love this quote by Anne Lamott about grace:

> I do not at all understand the mystery of grace—only that it meets us where we are but does not leave us where it found us.[3]

Grace is a change agent because it doesn't leave us without a home, an identity, or a place of safety and belonging. It doesn't leave us or our view of God unchanged.

Although our God does not change, I believe that our vision and experience of Him can grow as we do, not physically but spiritually, emotionally, and mentally. And, when our view of God expands, order is restored.

The Lord's presence is with His people. It has been that way from the beginning. The design of God's story, His vision, is to be with us. It was the order that God intended. This has not changed.

The story of humanity began amid God's presence, with His breath giving us life. As the story continued, God's presence was found in a burning bush, at the top of a mountain, and pillars of cloud and fire. Later, a dwelling place was built by God's people, in partnership with His detailed instructions, first as a tent and then as a temple.

In Nehemiah, God's holiness spread from the temple into the city of Jerusalem. It was the beginning of God's mission to reach all the nations.

God's presence came in human form next, as Jesus. It was Jesus who reiterated the words of God to the Israelites as they wandered through the desert—

> My presence will go with you [Come to me all who
> are weary and burdened], and I will give you
> rest.
>
> — EX 33:14, MATT 11:28

Now, as followers of Christ, we are filled with His presence and carry it with us wherever we go. This is part of our inheritance as God's sons and daughters. What matters is not what we know but that God knows us. That we can be held by Him. Our inheritance is part of our identity. Our inheritance is secure, immeasurable, and will never go away; it is being stored and kept for us. The Holy Spirit is our promise, the deposit for our inheritance—we have it now (Ephesians 1:14). It is this truth of the fullness of God's Spirit in us that we must work from, wrestle from, reason, and rebuild from.

In Christ is where we are, and it defines us. It's a place. A space to stay and dwell.

In the Gospel of John, Jesus talks about abiding. It makes

sense that He would, especially since, as a man, Jesus left His heavenly home to make His abode with humanity; in other words, He "moved into the neighborhood" (John 1:14, MSG). He was and is Immanuel, God with us.

Earlier, I wrote about Jesus calling Himself the "true vine" in John 15:1. Later in this same passage, He uses the word *abide* ten times in nine verses. Jesus also touches on the idea of "producing fruit." Jesus' message here is similar to the one in the parable of the sower/seeds; only the individual who remains in Jesus, the fertile soil, the true vine, and the Word of God (John 1:1), will produce fruit. The one who abides in Jesus and Jesus in Him will show evidence of this relationship.

The word for *abide* (*meno*) means to *stay in a given place, state, relation, or expectancy.* To remain. The word *fruit* (*karpos*) means *that which originates or comes from something*—the result of a relationship or connection.

What is interesting about grapevines is that they prefer rocky soil; I know this from experience. The fruit is evidence that the branches get what they need to thrive by staying connected to the vine. Whenever I tie up the heavy branches or pick a bunch of grapes from the vine in my backyard, I am reminded that the perfect conditions aren't always necessary to produce fruit. Sometimes, the opposite is true. Even when our own rocky soil makes us feel unsteady and the elements around us are harsh and overwhelming, we can make our home with Jesus as He makes His abode with us. Staying connected to the true vine will lead to fruit. That is the evidence that brings God glory and proves that we are disciples of Jesus (John 15:8). "Even in the unknowing of everything else, we can surely know Jesus."[4]

FINDING HOME IN JERUSALEM

Despite being under Roman rule, Jerusalem and its temple remained the holy city for the Jewish people until the temple's destruction in 70 A.D.[5] I don't know enough to debate or even speak on the holiness of Israel and/or Jerusalem presently. However, I do know that there is a promise of its complete restoration in the future.

The visions of the Apostle John in the final book of the Bible give us a description of what the *new* holy city will look like:

> *Then I saw "a new heaven and a new earth," for the first heaven and the first earth had passed away, and there was no longer any sea. I saw the Holy City, the new Jerusalem, coming down out of heaven from God, prepared as a bride beautifully dressed for her husband. And I heard a loud voice from the throne saying, "Look! God's dwelling place is now among the people, and He will dwell with them. They will be His people, and God himself will be with them and be their God. He will wipe every tear from their eyes. There will be no more death or mourning or crying or pain, for the old order of things has passed away." He who was seated on the throne said, "I am making everything new!"*
>
> — REVELATION 21:1-5

We have not been asked to do this life alone. To be faithful without the One who fills us with faith. To move forward without the One who plans our steps. Through the blood of Jesus, we have been given full access to a God who does not change. Who is infinite and abundant... in love, grace, mercy, and power. He will equip us. He is in us, and we are in Him.

It is your pain from today, your fear and your grief, your doubt and insecurity that Christ carried with Him to the cross. It was your sin from yesterday and tomorrow—the ones you're sorry for and those you don't even know about yet. Those are the ones He bore.

All of these were crushed with Him. He conquered them along with death. They have happened and will occur, yet they are all gone. He has already carried them and will carry them again if you allow Him to.

As we look forward to a time without pain, tears, and sin, we may be like the psalmist who said, "How lovely is your dwelling place, Lord Almighty" (Psalm 84:1)!

Rebuilding is not the end. Restoration is coming. For now, His presence is our good. We can be satisfied there. It's our home.

Reflection + Study Guide Questions

At the end of each chapter, ask yourself, "Now that I've read this chapter:

1. What do I know about God?
2. What do I know about myself and my identity?
3. What do I know about belonging?
4. What did I learn about home?

INTRODUCTION

1. Describe "home." What does it look like? Feel like? Etc.

CHAPTER 1: BEFORE THE WORDS

1. What is the story God has been writing for you? When have you felt His absence? When have you known His presence?

CHAPTER 2: REBUILDING BEGINS WITH A BURDEN

1. What did this chapter reveal to you about the word "empty"?
2. Who are your people? Where are your places? What is your burden?
3. How has shame overwhelmed you? What does it look like for you to allow God to overwhelm you instead?

CHAPTER 3: OPPORTUNITY FOR CHANGE

1. What did this chapter reveal to you about the word "overwhelmed"?
2. What would it look like for you to seek God's vision for your rebuilding?
3. What from your past might God be asking you to give up?
4. What is keeping you from moving forward and surrendering your future? How does your bravery inspire others? How does it show them that you know and love Jesus?
5. What has overwhelmed or overtaken your identity?

CHAPTER 4: EVALUATE THE RUBBLE

1. What did this chapter reveal to you about the word "breathe"?
2. Create a timeline of your life to this point. Where have you been? Where are you now? Where do you want to go?
3. What is a story you have been telling yourself? What lies, doubts, shame, or distractions have crept in and

crowded out the voice of God that says, "It is very good"?

4. What has God already revealed to you about who you are?

CHAPTER 5: REBUILDING IN COMMUNITY

1. What did this chapter reveal to you about the word "deep"?
2. Are you allowing God to move beyond your expectations? Surrender your expectations. Receive expectancy.
3. What do you need help with in your current season? Who are the helpers in your life?
4. Is there anyone you trust to hold you accountable as you move toward health and healing?
5. You might not see the "final" product of rebuilding in your lifetime. What type of inheritance are you leaving for future generations?

CHAPTER 6: WORK + FIGHT GO TOGETHER

1. What did this chapter reveal to you about the word "remember"?
2. The opportunity to rebuild is here. Are you ready or resistant? What is at stake if you allow the opposition to win? What is at stake if you don't move forward and rebuild?
3. What or who is your biggest adversary (e.g., lies you believe, mindset, circumstances, etc.)? What weapons (or resources) do you have to fight?
4. How will you remember what God has done in the past to help you with the present? Your future?

5. How is the enemy trying to distract you from God's story in you? Is it based on your identity, mission/purpose, or through suffering, etc.?

CHAPTER 7: REBUILDING REVEALS VULNERABILITY + HOPE

1. What did this chapter reveal to you about the word "believe"?
2. Are you living out of a place where you believe God is who He says He is?
3. In what ways do I need to reorient to God? To begin again?
4. What is holding you back? What do you need to release so that you can take hold of hope? What are the habits, attitudes, thoughts, etc., that are no longer serving you in this season?
5. How are you using your privilege to help others more vulnerable than you?

CHAPTER 8: EMBRACE LIMITS AND CELEBRATE

1. What did this chapter reveal to you about the word "boundary"?
2. What do you think disqualifies you from the kindness of the Lord?
3. Which of your limitations is God asking you to embrace? What does that look like practically?
4. What does it look like for you to be rooted in Christ but also to move beyond your boundaries?
5. Sometimes to build into the new, confession is necessary. Pray and ask God to search you and lead you in the direction of confession, if necessary.

CHAPTER 9: REMEMBERING LEADS TO SURRENDER

1. What did this chapter reveal to you about the word "freedom"?
2. List ways God has been faithful to you, even in your days, months, or years of hardship. Thank Him for His faithfulness.
3. In what ways has God brought light to your darkest places? How has He brought freedom where there has only been slavery?
4. What do you need to exchange?

CHAPTER 10: NEW BEGINNINGS + COMMITMENTS

1. What did this chapter reveal to you about the word "stand"?
2. What dream would you bring to fruition if you knew you couldn't fail? If you had no limitations?
3. Name each of your broken places and offer them to God for healing. Do the same for your places of longing.

CHAPTER 11: REBUILDING IS ONGOING + WE ARE BEING BUILT

1. What did this chapter reveal to you about the word "behold"?
2. Do you believe in a God who transforms you every minute of every day?
3. In what ways do you desire comfort over safety? The temporary over the eternal?

CHAPTER 12: THE FINAL WORDS + WORDS YET TO COME

1. What do you know about God now that will keep you abiding in Him as you rebuild into the new?
2. What does the hope of restoration mean to you? What would it look like for you to allow it to bring you hope in your rebuilding?

Notes

CHAPTER 2

1. Kathleen B Neilson, *Knowing the Bible: Ezra and Nehemiah, A 12-Week Study* (Wheaton, IL: Crossway, 2016), 8

CHAPTER 3

1. Brennan Manning, *Abba's Child* (Colorado Springs, CO: NavPress, 1994), 146-147 (kindle edition)
2. Christie Purifoy, *Roots and Sky* (Grand Rapids, MI: Revell, 2016), 173
3. Annie Downs (host), "Episode 119: Scott Sauls", January 24, 2019, *That Sounds Fun* (podcast)
4. Daniel L Smith-Christopher, *Theological Bible Commentary*, (Louisville, KY: Westminster John Knox Press, 2021), 161
5. Smith, Angie, February 2016 (IF: Gathering)

CHAPTER 4

1. Kat Armstrong, Mountains: *Rediscovering your Vision and Restoring your Hope in God's Presence* (Colorado Springs, CO: NavPress, 2023), 27
2. *Ibid.* 16

CHAPTER 5

1. Jamie Ivey (host), *The Happy Hour with Jamie Ivey* (podcast), June 2016

2. *Toy Story 4.* Pixar, June 2019

3. Victor P Hamilton, Handbook on the Historical Books (Grand Rapids, MI: Baker Academic, 2004), 507

CHAPTER 6

1. Michael Jackson, Lyrics to "The Girl is Mine", Performed by Michael Jackson and Paul McCartney, Epic, 1982 https://en.wikipedia.org/wiki/The_Girl_Is_Mine

2. Richard Rohr, *Everything Belongs: The Gift of Contemplative Prayer* (New York, NY: The Crossroad Publishing Company, 2003), 54-55

CHAPTER 8

1. C.S. Lewis, *A Grief Observed* (New York, NY: Harper Collins Publishers, 1961), 60

2. Aubrey Sampson, The Louder Song (Colorado Springs, CO: NavPress, 2019), 54

3. John Mark Comer, "The Power of Margin in a World Without Limits," Bridgetown Church, 12/1/19 https://podcasts.apple.com/us/podcast/the-power-of-margin-in-a-world-without-limits/id84246334?i=1000458472925

4. Dr. Thomas L Constable, "Notes on Nehemiah, 2023," Plano Bible Chapel (website) https://www.planobiblechapel.org/tcon/notes/html/ot/nehemiah/nehemiah.htm

5. Priscilla Shirer, *The Armor of God* (Nashville, TN: LifeWay Church Resources, 2015), 8-36

6. Russ Ramsey, *Advent of the Lamb of God* (Downers Grove, IL: InterVarsity Press, 2018), 76-77

7. C. Austin Miles, Lyrics to "In the Garden", 1913 https://hymnary.org/text/i_come_to_the_garden_alone

CHAPTER 9

1. Let's Make a Deal (game show), https://www.cbs.com/shows/lets_make_a_deal/
2. Dr. Thomas L Constable, "Notes on Nehemiah," *Plano Bible Chapel* (website), 2023 https://www.planobiblechapel.org/tcon/notes/html/ot/nehemiah/nehemiah.html

CHAPTER 10

1. Meg Bucher, "Who was Mary Magdalene in the Bible?", *Bible Study Tools* (website), February 2, 2023 https://www.biblestudytools.com/bible-study/topical-studies/who-was-mary-magdalene.html
2. *Ibid.*
3. Gordon J Wenham, *The Book of Leviticus* (Grand Rapids, MI: Wm. B. Eerdmans Publishing Co., 1979), 95
4. Jenn Jett Barrett, February 2023 (Camp Well for Leaders)

CHAPTER 11

1. Rachel Held Evans, *Searching for Sunday* (Nashville, TN: Nelson Books, 2015), 19
2. Sybil Kolbert, *A Place at the Table* (Fresno, CA: Sybil Kolbert, 2017), 44-46
3. Banning Liebscher, *Rooted* (New York, NY: Waterbrook Press, 2016), 121
4. Jennie Allen, *Nothing to Prove* (New York, NY: Waterbrook Press, 2017), 74
5. Dru Johnson, Human Rites (Grand Rapids, MI: Wm B Eerdmans Publishing Co., 2019), 59

CHAPTER 12

1. Jennifer Gaeng, "How Long Do Hermit Crabs Live?", A-Z Animals (website), January 2022, https://a-z-animals.com/blog/hermit-crab-lifespan-how-long-do-hermit-crabs-live/

2. Ben Lutkevich, "change agent (agent of change)", *TechTarget* (website), https://www.techtarget.com/searchcio/definition/change-agent

3. Anne Lamott, *Traveling Mercies* (New York, NY: Pantheon Books, 1999), 146

4. Emily P Freeman (host), The Next Right Thing (podcast)

5. R. A. Batey, "Jerusalem", *Dictionary of New Testament Background* (Downers Grove, IL: InterVarsity Press, 2000), 559-561

All definitions of English words were taken from: Merriam-Webster Dictionary https://www.merriam-webster.com. *Merriam-Webster's Dictionary of English Usage. Springfield, Mass. :Merriam-Webster, Inc., 1994.*

All translations of English text into Greek and Hebrew were taken from: Interlinear Bible at https://biblehub.com/interlinear

Additional Resources

Tremper Longman III and Raymond B. Dillard, *An Introduction to the Old Testament* (Grand Rapids, MI: Zondervan Academic, 2006)

Kelly Minter, *Nehemiah: A Heart that Can Break* (audio sessions) (Nashville, TN: Lifeway Christian Resources, 2012)

Douglas J. E. Nykolaishen and Andrew J. Schmutzer, *Ezra, Nehemiah, and Esther (Teach the Text Commentary Series)* (Grand Rapids, MI: Baker Books, 2018)

Warren Wiersbe, *Be Determined* (Colorado Springs, CO: David C Cook, 1992)